Realistic
Home Businesses

Make Money Now With Your Own Home Business

Pat D. SLOSS

Copyright © 2012 Pat D. Sloss

Pat D. Sloss
http://www.pdsloss.com
http://www.realistichomebusinesses.com

Realistic Press
Falcon, Colorado
http://www.realisticpress.com

Realistic Home Businesses

Edited by Louise Killifer and Shirley Fox
Cover illustration by J.W. Peck II
Printed in the U.S.A.

DISCLAIMER AND/OR LEGAL NOTICES
While the author has made every effort to provide accurate information and Internet addresses at the time of publication, neither the publisher or author assume any responsibility for errors or for changes that occur after publication. The information presented represents the view of the author at the date of publication.

ISBN: 0985453702
ISBN-13: 978-0-9854537-0-1

Dedication

To all who started to give up on their dreams of self employment but decided to give it one more try.

To my parents for their constant love, support, and guidance. They taught me the importance of hard work , faith, and that big dreams were possible. I was always taught "you can do it." Their lessons will never be forgotten.

To my friends for their constant support.

Table of contents

Acknowledgments

No book is ever written without the help and encouragement of others. I want to thank the following people for all they have done to help and encourage me. I am so lucky to have such long term friends who have been an integral part of this book and my life.

I would like to thank my friend J.W. Peck II for designing the illustration for the cover of this book. We have been friends since we were 7 years old. Thank you for your willingness to do this job on such short notice and create exactly what I wanted.

Thanks to my two editors, Louise Killifer, who I have known since I was 7 years old and Shirley Fox, who I met in my 20's. Both of them invested countless hours editing and discussing the concepts of this book. I am grateful not only for their time and editing skills, but also their long term friendship. Both of them went way beyond the extra mile in helping me with this book.

Thank you to my friend Kay Wilcox who has patiently listened to all of my ideas and supported me in many ways. Her experiences helped create ideas for part of this book. I met Kay in my 20's. She helps keep me on track when I wander off.

A big thanks to my many other friends and acquaintances who gave me the inspiration and ideas to write this book. They may not have known it, but they said just the right thing at the right time. It would be hard to measure how much other people influence our lives and the good they do.

Chapter 1

Real Work at Home Opportunities

One of the most important areas of your life is finding the right job or business for you. Your choice of the right job, business or career will have more of an impact on the quality of your life than almost anything you do, other than selecting your spouse. There are more than 100,000 possible job categories in the U.S. You must do your homework well on the selection of starting your own business.

Would you like to work for yourself? Any job, service, or hobby you have ever done successfully, can be an idea for your own business. I have used hobbies and previous job experiences to start several of my own successful businesses. There are also opportunities that you can easily learn to do that would make a great work at home business. Use this book to discover your new business and do something you enjoy.

The ideas in this book are not work at home scam jobs like stuffing envelopes or making baby clothes, but real opportunities, making real money. In some instances, with little training, you can make a very good income. I imagine many of you have tried or at least sent for information on some of the opportunities that ask for money from you, just so you can try their scam. This book lists only real business prospects and gives you the guidance to brainstorm to find your own calling if your specific opportunity is not listed in the book. I will note the businesses I have personally tried or friends have started, and the financial outcome. You can then take any business in this book and put your special twist on it to make the perfect home business for you. The purpose is to give you enough ideas that you can find your perfect niche.

More than half of all U.S. businesses are based out of an owner's home or started in the home. Apple Computer, Hershey's, Ford Motor, Hewlett Packard and Mary Kay Cosmetics all started out as home based businesses. I was previously an engineer for Hewlett Packard and I was inspired when I heard the history of Hewlett Packard starting in a garage. If companies that have become a huge success can start at home in a spare room or garage, then it is possible for all of us. Money was even tighter in the 1930's, than it is now, when Bill Hewlett and David Packard started Hewlett Packard in a garage. It was that inspiration that made me begin my quest for part-time and home based businesses.

The Internet has provided more ways to sell services and products that did not exist years ago. Now, business opportunities reach worldwide. Choose the type of work, part-time or full-time, and the amount of money you would like to make. How hard are you willing to work to make it happen? You may end up working long hours to begin, but wouldn't it be worth it to do something you enjoy? On the other hand, you may just want a part-time business to supplement your income.

There are several types of work at home or work out of your home opportunities. It is my mission to tell you about numerous businesses you can operate from your home or vehicle. This book will help you select the business that will fit your purpose and personality. The other chapters will tell you how to get started and ideas to set up the business. There are also part-time and temporary opportunities that you could use for additional income.

Let's face it, in this economy, there are many people out of work, and many others who are under employed. Many are working several part-time jobs and barely making ends meet. The fuel, clothing and food (if you have to eat out) for some of these part-time jobs can really bite into any salary made from working.

In today's job market, employers have thousands of resumes on their desk. Thousands are literally thrown out because there are so many. It is almost impossible to get through the screening process. When there are thousands of people looking at one job opportunity, you don't have very good odds. Selling yourself to get a job is difficult to do, whereas selling services or products is much easier. Marketing yourself is not only easier but faster. You do not have to have permission from anyone but yourself. It is much easier to sell your services or products to people who want them. People will come to you.

Starting slow takes the pressure off. You can develop your skills and start with a part-time business. You may find you have all of the skills already that you need to start your business. If you need additional skills, try taking online or in person classes. There are even some free online classes available. Many of these opportunities cost little or nothing to start. Remember, Bill Gates was only a high school graduate and Thomas Edison had a sixth grade education.

Transition from an 8-5 job to entrepreneur may be a little frightening but the security of a job is all in the mind. Layoffs from jobs happen all the time, the higher you move up, the more miserable you can become or more at risk for a layoff. Some companies have laid off 30 to 50 percent of their workers, while others cease to even exist. Having a job is the illusion of security.

It is said that having a job is safer than being an entrepreneur but an entrepreneur usually has multiple sources of income from multiple clients. If they lose one client, they still have others and some income left. If you lose a job, your entire income goes to zero.

Many times friends and family say to play it safe and stay in a job or look for another job. Rise above negativity and understand where they are coming from. Most all of us have been programmed to have a job. We assume having a job is safe and secure, however in this economy, a suitable job may be difficult to find. Some are still diligently searching after 3 years.   They say it is too risky to start a business.

Do not hang around negative people. Try to spend time with like-minded friends and family that will support your ideas. Even when negative talk is directed toward you or your new business ideas, don't take it personally. Negativity is basically selfishness, and their selfishness is about them, not about you. Try to remain objective and assess whether their is any rational basis for the criticism. You could have missed a point you need to research or the other person might be wishing they could be starting a new business. We all know people that would not be happy if you handed them a one hundred dollar bill.

It is my wish to give you enough information to decide if working at home is right for you. This information will help you identify your passion(s) and recognize previous experience that could be useful in a business of your own. In addition, you will determine your level of motivation from the suggested opportunity types. You will learn how to set up your new business and will be given general structures and tax implications of self-employment.   I have also included information on each opportunity to inform you about what steps to take next and where to find additional information.

You will be given lot of information on work opportunities, however you must do your own research on the type of work you select. Consider your location, access to the Internet, computer proficiency and understanding, and if there is a local outlet to sell your services or products.   Services and/or products can be sold locally or online. The following chapters will help you decide what is right for you and how to approach a home based business. Start today, do something positive.

NOTE: Please refer to my websites for business resources, books, courses, software, equipment and supplies for the businesses in this book. From time to time additional business opportunities will be posted on my website. I hope this information makes the research for your new business easier. Clicking on the links in the websites will take you to resources for each item.

http://www.pdsloss.com/
http://www.RealisticHomeBusinesses.com/

Chapter 2

Finding Work That Matches Your Skills and Passions

This chapter will help you identify your skills and passions. You may have forgotten or buried some of your passions while you were too busy looking for any job that would pay the bills. We may not acknowledge all of our abilities until we think about all we have accomplished. Let's jump right in and make a list.

List all of your past jobs and hobbies and the skills it took to accomplish each one. You may be surprised to see how many there actually are on your list. If you don't want to mark up the book, make your lists on notebook paper and keep it handy to write on as things pop into your head.

Skills

1.
2.
3.
4.
5.
6.
7.
8.
9.
10.
11.

12.
13.
14.
15.
16.
17.
18.
19.
20.
21.
22.
23.
24.
25.
26.
27.
28.
29.
30.

Now list your passions. These passions might be things you may have left behind years ago or interests you still have. List anything like music, crafts, causes, or artistic endeavors...anything you have or had a passion to try.

Passions

1.
2.
3.
4.
5.
6.
7.
8.

9.
10.
11.
12.
13.
14.
15.
16.
17.
18.
19.
20.

This process may surprise you. You may not have enough lines for all of the skills and passions. Pick the top five skills and mark your five most important passions. Everyone is different but you should get some idea of what you would like to do with your passions and what are your best skills. Do your top skills and passions spark any long forgotten ideas? It is OK if no ideas come to mind yet. We have more work to do to decide on a direction or number of directions where your interests lie. Even though you may already have a particular type of business in mind, these lists may help you drill down on the subjects and help you find a niche you have not thought of before.

Narrow your search by selecting your preferences on the following list of different kinds of work. You may be restricted physically or your personality may dictate some kinds of work that you may be better at than others. Select your preferences from the following list.

- Indoors
- Outdoors
- Mix of indoors and outdoors
- On your feet
- Physical stamina

- Deskwork
- Telephone work
- Face to face
- Solitary
- Little or no contact with customer
- Work directly with customers
- Need staff
- Part time
- Full time
- Work at home
- Work from home
- Work at customer's location
- Travel involved
- Geographically transferable (you can take the business with you and live most anywhere)
- Consulting
- Contract work
- Job to job
- Wholesale
- Retail
- Inventory required
- Franchise

You should be getting a picture of the type of business you might want. Now, lets do an exercise on skills. Pick the skills you have. If you are missing one skill or just not as proficient as you would like to be, you can easily take a class online or at a local college to update computer skills, spreadsheets or word processing.

- Trade skills (i.e. electrician)
- Computer
- Bookkeeping
- Technical
- Equipment
- Software

- Hardware
- Artistic
- Social Media

List any skills you need to learn or update. You do not need to be able to do everything yourself unless you are a one person show. Family members may be able to fill in with their skills. You may need to enlist the help of a bookkeeper if that is not one of your skills. Keeping good books is a very important business function that you need to learn.

Now make a list of your top five skills, top five passions, work preferences, and skills you need to learn or update. A picture of your new business should be forming. Next, see if working at home or working from home is really for you.

NOTE: Please refer to my websites for business resources, books, courses, software, equipment and supplies for the businesses in this book.   From time to time additional business opportunities will be posted on my website. I hope this information makes the research for your new business easier. Clicking on the links in the websites will take you to resources for each item.

http://www.pdsloss.com/
http://www.RealisticHomeBusinesses.com/

Chapter 3

Is Working At Home Right For You

Before making any major changes and/or investing money in a new endeavor, make sure working at home is right for you. Working at home takes a lot of self-motivation. Do you have what it takes? Advantages and disadvantages are listed below. Think about the list and make sure there is not a deal breaker listed.

Advantages:

- Can start part time
- Additional or replacement income
- Possible substantial increase in income
- Flexible work hours
- More flexible lifestyle
- More family time
- Lower start-up and operating costs than a rented office or space
- Cost savings on child care
- No commuting
- Savings on clothing and meals out
- Satisfaction of being own boss and enjoying your work
- Increased tax benefits and write-offs
- Outlet for creative/unique talents
- Possible employment of family members

Disadvantages:

- Your home may lack space needed for business and family use
- Lack of benefits...health, disability, retirement and vacation
- Possible long work hours
- You must have the motivation to keep working when at home
- Personal and family lifestyle patterns may be disturbed
- Business and family privacy may be disrupted
- Lack of social interaction
- Lack of opportunities to network
- Stress balancing family and business in the same space
- Family members and friends may not understand you can't be interrupted when working, even though you are at home
- Some business activities may cause problems with neighbors
- Zoning may prohibit some activities

Having the support of family members and friends is extremely important to the success of your business. Family members should be able to share their thoughts and give input on new business plans. Starting a new business at home will be a big change to you and family members, not only time and space, but also schedules. Be sure to pay attention how this change will affect not only you, but also the rest of your family. Look carefully at the advantages and disadvantages to make sure working at home is right for you. Try to limit business hours to specific times of the day and week. Allow time for family vacations and for leisure entertainment activities. You may have to work some unusual or long hours from time to time, but leaving time for other activities is important. Keep a clear distinction between business time and family time. Make sure that family and friends understand that just because you are home, you cannot be interrupted or do all of the household chores and work. Make sure you do not take on too much business if you have young children. You can consider operating part time if you have young children. Then you can take on more work as the children grow older.

Part-time or Full-time Business

Do you want a full-time business or to just earn extra income on a part-time basis? Many of the opportunities in this book will work for either full-time or part-time businesses but others are strictly full-time.

Space

Do you have the room in your home for an office? You really need a separate space of some sort where regular household interruptions will not bother you. You could even consider framing in an office in your garage if you could have electricity, heat and cooling if needed. While it is not impossible, a kitchen table business is not a great idea. A corner of a bedroom might be the worst idea. You cannot relax and go to sleep easily if you see a pile of unfinished work on a desk. If at all possible, keep work and family space separate.

First, you must choose the type of work to decide how much room you need to dedicate. Some businesses require a small office while others need shipping, storage, and inventory space. You may need to invest in a van or specialized vehicle. There are tax consequences and deductions that you will need to be aware of and decide on before or soon after you start your business. The business use of your vehicle requires good bookkeeping since you can take a mileage deduction or depreciate the vehicle and use actual expenses. Personal use versus business use must also be decided. Some of your decisions for tax purposes cannot be changed so make sure you make the right decision in the beginning.

NOTE: Please refer to my websites for business resources, books, courses, software, equipment and supplies for the businesses in this book.   From time to time additional business opportunities will be posted on my website. I hope this information makes the research for your new business easier. Clicking on the links in the websites will take you to resources for each item.

http://www.pdsloss.com/
http://www.RealisticHomeBusinesses.com/

Chapter 4

Types Of Work and Scams to Avoid

There are three main types of work at home opportunities.

1. Self-employed working for yourself

2. Consultant working from contract to contract

3. Telecommute working for an employer

The next three chapters will describe each opportunity and a good description of each business or opportunity.

Each type of opportunity fits certain personality types. You should not try to be self-employed if you do not have the motivation to be a self-starter. It is very easy to find all kinds of interruptions at home to stall off work. If you have motivation issues, you might prefer telecommuting or at least working contract to contract. That way a job has a deadline that you must meet. You must set your own deadlines when working for yourself and be motivated and dedicated enough to stick to a schedule.

Self Employed Working for Yourself

Self employment opportunities will be listed in the next chapter. There are many more opportunities but the list in this book is different than many books and the idea is to find your niche. Your niche might be a combination or one part of one of the listed ideas. Chapter 8 will deal more on finding your niche if you are not finding quite what you want in the next three chapters. Self employment may also contain a certain amount of consulting but normally for very short-time jobs.

Consultant Working from Contract to Contract

Job Shop Consulting. Consulting from contract to contract might be considered as self-employment but you would be working for one employer for the duration of a contract or job. It might depend on how the contract is structured. I did consulting work for several "job shop" agencies. Businesses can use a job shop agency to furnish employees. Under those circumstances the employer is not responsible for any benefits, payroll or unemployment. The job shop hires you to work on someone's contract. The business gets to test your abilities with no commitments. This is often used in aerospace to hire electrical engineers, writers, illustrators, mechanical engineers, and support people. You normally get a higher rate, but are responsible for your own benefits. If you work for the job shop long enough, they will sometimes offer reduced health benefits and a few other perks. Eventually, the company may want to hire you permanently if they like you and you fit the job they want to fill.

Consult Directly. Consider consulting for yourself and deal directly with the company or person you will work for. I have also done engineering consulting in this manner. This is actually better than working for a job shop since you eliminate the middle man. You will need good negotiation skills to get the salary you want. You will also have to furnish your own benefits in this type of job situation so make sure the contract salary is good enough that you can purchase your own health insurance and make up other benefits you would have at a captive job.

Telecommute for an Employer

Telecommuting is not really your own home business but does allow you to work at home which might be the next best thing to your own business. Telecommuting for an employer usually requires that you work for the employer for a specified time in their offices. The company wants to know if you can do the job and they need to trust that you will be able to do that job at home before they turn you loose. The number of companies that allow employees to telecommute is growing. It saves them office space and they also know that many people get more accomplished at home. There are many less distractions. There are no coffee pots to gossip over and the bathroom is much closer. Gone are many of the interruptions you have when working in an office environment. I personally worked for an employer who allowed me to telecommute. I found that I produced more work at home than in the office, mostly due to the distractions and meetings of the office environment that I did not have at home.

A list of the companies known for allowing employees to telecommute is listed in Chapter 7. You may have to gain their trust first or you may already work for a company who will allow you to telecommute. Some allow almost full-time telecommuting and others three to four days a week. It not only saves you commuting, lunches, and clothing but also saves your company productive time and office space.

Popular Work at Home Scams

The number of scam jobs are rapidly rising. With so many people out of work, the job market is a lucrative business for unethical scammers. The Internet is the perfect place for these scammers to find victims.

Watch for any of the following phrases or headlines and steer clear of any of the scam jobs. A sure tipoff is that you are required to pay a fee. You should be paid to do a job, not have to pay the company you work for. The fees are disguised as fees associated with materials they are sending to you, processing fees, intake fees, or to show you are serious about the opportunity. There may be a few exceptions for jobs for virtual call centers as far as training, background or credit checks. Some of these companies hire agents as independent contractors rather than employees. IRS regulations require companies to treat independent contractors differently than employees. See the IRS regulations when in question.

When "Work at Home" appears in the job headline, check for a scam. Most real jobs start with the job title, bookkeeper, writer, etc.

Another tip off of scams is when either "no experience necessary" or "no resume required" are in the job listing. Typically, an employer wants a resume and experience.

If the job offer comes in your email as spam and looks like a great opportunity, beware. Spam is just a cheap method to reach many victims. Move this email to the trash and delete. Do not click on the "remove or unsubscribe" link. When you click on these links, you have just confirmed that your email address is active and you will probably get even more spam. Also beware if there is a claim of large paychecks, no job description, or a limited number of openings.

Do not give personal information during an application process. If you are asked for your social security number, bank account number, or a credit card number, end the conversation. You will need to give out your social security number for legitimate jobs, but not during the initial discussions. If you are going to be a consultant, get an EIN, also known as a federal tax number, from the IRS. This way, employers or multiple employers will not require your social security number. See Chapter 15 to learn how to apply for this number. It is a simple online procedure and will protect your privacy. You can also apply by mail. Any employer who pays you over a certain dollar amount (at present $600 per year) is supposed to furnish you with a 1099 miscellaneous income form at the end of the year. The EIN can be used for this purpose. At present, all you need is one EIN, even if you change the name of your business. The IRS ties the EIN number to your social security number.

Under no circumstances, fall for any of these job scams: check cashing/forwarding, data entry, surveys, package forwarding, rebate processing, envelope stuffing, and most mystery shopping opportunities. Also beware of opportunities that look real from real companies but with contacts using the free e-mail addresses of Hotmail, Gmail, etc.

To investigate offers, check the company out with the better business bureau and/or search online using the company name followed by a "+" and "scam."   Many times you will be able to see a long list of complaints.

Check your "gut feeling." If it makes you uncomfortable or just does not feel right, then it is probably a scam. Check and recheck any offer that you find online.

NOTE: Please refer to my websites for business resources, books, courses, software, equipment and supplies for the businesses in this book.   From time to time additional business opportunities will be posted on my website. I hope this information makes the research for your new business easier. Clicking on the links in the websites will take you to resources for each item.

http://www.pdsloss.com/
http://www.RealisticHomeBusinesses.com/

Chapter 5

Self Employment Tips

There may be a lot of people who want to discourage you from working at home. They will have all kinds of negative comments about why it will not work and that you will fail.   This can make you start to have some doubts and affect your momentum.

Dealing With Negative People

When you explain the positive side of working at home, others may be interested in knowing how they could also work at home. Explain the positives such as, no commuting expenses, savings on clothing, not having to deal with coworkers or bosses as often, more personal/family time due to no commuting, savings on meals out, increased tax benefits and write-offs, more flexible work hours, and an increase in income.

Time Management

Working at home takes a lot of self-motivation. There are some people who are not able to stay motivated, nor can they take the isolation.   Most of us could use some time management help. Limit your time checking emails. If you can, have a dedicated email address and phone number just for work. Inform all of your friends you will be working and can't be interrupted between certain hours, unless it is an emergency. Some people think if you work at home you can do anything you want and/or chat on the phone or in person. Be very firm with these people. It does not matter if you are working for another company or for yourself, you cannot afford to fritter your time away. If a company found out you were supposed to be working for them and were really having coffee with your buddy, it would be grounds to be fired or your telecommuting privileges discontinued. If you are working for yourself, you will cause your business to fail if you do not manage your time properly. If you have the motivation but do not like isolation, then select a home business that will put you in front of your customers such as a service business.

Invest in a day planner and write down your daily and weekly schedule. You may need to refer to your planner to see when you talked to a customer, have an appointment, or a deadline. Write down the tasks or appointments for each day to stay organized. Keep good records since you may also need this information for tax purposes. You can also keep your car mileage and expense information for supplies in the day planner.

Try to check emails only at certain times of the day. If you leave your personal email program open, you will be tempted to check your email to see the message. Creating separate e-mail accounts for work related and personal emails is a must. Keep your personal email program turned off while you are working and only check it at certain times of the day. If you do business with people in different time zones or countries, keep a time zone clock on your favorites or bookmarks list.

Your Office

Make a budget for your business plan. Don't go into debt to furnish your home office. In the beginning, get the basics. A desk you already have or a Goodwill desk will work fine if you are on a tight budget. I would rather spend money on bringing money in rather than on furniture. Save your receipts in a shoebox, if nothing else since you will need them for tax deduction purposes. When you start making money, you can buy nicer office furniture. All business purchases should be entered in the bookkeeping system of your choice. Do not wait until the end of the year.

Computer

You may have a computer you can use, but if not, watch for the sales on a computer that will do the job you need. Obviously a graphic designer or photographer will need a high-end computer. Someone who will do invoicing, write letters and do limited bookkeeping can use a lower end computer. If you do high-end work, a desktop computer is preferable. You have more options for high quality graphic cards, hard drives and memory with a desktop. If you travel and will need a computer on the trip, you will need a laptop.

The laptop computers are catching up with desktop computers and many people use them fulltime. I have found that a laptop is great, other than the mouse and keyboard. I normally plug in a full size keyboard and regular mouse. However ridiculous it may sound, I found a lightweight folding vinyl or rubber keyboard that looks like a toy but is perfect for traveling and so much easier than the laptop keyboard to use. You can find them online or at some local businesses and they fold or roll up. A regular keyboard is of course best but you may be pressed for space if traveling. A mouse is a must have item for me, even if I have to use the laptop keyboard for a while. I just cannot get used to the touch pad in place of a mouse. Travel sized mice are available and they are about half the size of a regular mouse. You would not want to use the small size all day since they are a little more awkward and tedious to use than the large size and might cause carpel tunnel syndrome. Personal preference and the availability of options for your computer will be the deciding factor for you.

For the best of all worlds, buy a high end laptop and connect it to a docking station when at home. A docking station lets you connect to a larger monitor, keyboard, mouse, printer, scanner and more without having to connect all of the cables directly to the laptop. When you are going on a trip, you only have to disconnect one cable from the docking station and you are ready to go. The high end laptop gives you a better video card, more memory, a larger hard drive, and sometimes better quality overall. You can upgrade a low end for more memory etc. but by the time you are finished, it will cost the same or more. If your business in not that dependent on a computer, you can buy a low end computer of either type and do just fine.

All-in-One: Printer, Copier, Scanner, and Fax

You may need a printer, scanner and a fax. There are all-in-one machines that are very reasonable for just slightly over $100.00. The price could be even better during a sale.

If a second phone line for faxing is a problem, there are online services that provide fax services with your own 800 number, at a very reasonable rate per month. The rate is tied to the number of faxes per month. You connect to the service online, read your faxes and save or print on your printer. That kind of service is much cheaper than a dedicated phone line, a fax machine, and ink. This allows you to save a copy of all of your faxes. You can send a fax through the service in the same way, on your computer. The only problem comes when you want to fax something you did not create on your computer like a picture. The solution is to scan and save to a file on your computer in order to fax through the service on your computer.

If you buy an all-in-one printer you can scan anything from pictures to text. Even if you don't use the fax portion of an all-in-one, the print, copy, and scan functions are very worthwhile. The ability to make copies is also very important. Many of the fax machines will also hook up to your only phone line and you can set them to answer if they hear a fax tone when your answering machine picks up a call after four rings. They will normally not work if you have an answering service connected with your phone company.

Your Office Space

It is important to keep your office organized, clean, and neat. Most businesses should have at least a small filing cabinet, a desk, computer, and a printer. Your office should be in a quiet spot away from any family living spaces. If you have small children, you may want a lockable space. If you were working on an important editing or contract job and a child started playing with the computer when you stepped out or were gone, it could be a disaster.

Managing People and Pets

Try to work when others are out of the house. If you have younger children, arrange to have someone watch them while you are working, just as if you were working outside your home. It is not professional to have a screaming, crying child in the background while you are on the phone with an important client. A client would think twice about hiring someone with a ruckus going on, wondering how well you could concentrate on their job. Children would normally be in school but if they are home while you are working, you must make it clear to them you will be on important phone calls and should not be disturbed except for an emergency. Neighbors and friends also need to be told what your working hours are and that you cannot be disturbed other than for an emergency. When I was working at home, some friends thought it was an opportunity to call and chat. You have to make them understand that they cannot call when you are working, unless it is an emergency.

Combating Isolation

There are times you will feel lonely and isolated. A good way to combat isolation is to leave in your car during the lunch hour and meet friends for lunch or go to a store. Another idea is to go for a walk in the park. When I did this, I came back refreshed and ready to finish my work. One temptation however, is to overstay the lunch hour. Manage your time like you were working a job and do not become distracted. One of the joys of working for yourself, however, is that you can take off half a day now and then.

NOTE: Please refer to my websites for business resources, books, courses, software, equipment and supplies for the businesses in this book.   From time to time additional business opportunities will be posted on my website. I hope this information makes the research for your new business easier. Clicking on the links in the websites will take you to resources for each item.

> http://www.pdsloss.com/
> http://www.RealisticHomeBusinesses.com/

Chapter 6

Agency Consultant, Contract to Contract

There are a number of jobs available as a consultant or contract to contract through temporary employment agencies. This type of work is generally called job shopping. You are interviewed and hired by the employment agency. You go to work at the company that needs the employee. The company pays the employment agency and the agency pays you whatever wage has been agreed upon.

The company and the agency have a contract to furnish an employee at a set amount. The agency makes its money on the difference between the company payment and the salary they pay you. This salary is sometimes set, at least for a time frame, but sometimes you can negotiate a higher salary if you have more experience or skills than someone else.

Companies love this agreement since they do not have to pay benefits or have any responsibility for unemployment for you and they can see if you are the employee they want to hire full time. They may only have a three month to one year job available and are hesitant to hire a full-time employee. It is also a good opportunity for you, hence the term, job shopping. You can see if you would like to work for the company full time. Your employer is actually the agency but you are "shopped out" to the company needing the work.

You will be required to sign a contract with the agency that you agree to not hire on direct with the company you are doing the work for until an agreed upon time frame has lapsed. This time frame is normally three to six months. The contract will also contain your wage amount, the time period when you will be paid, and if they will furnish any benefits. Normally if you work for a job shop for over 6 months, you will be offered some benefits such as health insurance. You will normally have to pay for these benefits but not near what they would cost if you bought them on your own since you would be part of a group. Read the contract carefully and ask questions if there is anything you do not understand. Each agency will have their own contract. You may be able to negotiate some of the terms like salary, length of commitment, health care, vacation, etc.

It is not possible to list all of the agencies since they will be specific to your area and go in and out of business. Some of the jobs listed online are through these agencies. Temporary jobs provide an entry into the workforce, supplemental income, and a bridge to full-time employment for many workers. When looking online or in the yellow pages, the temporary employment agencies may not use the word "temporary" in their heading and they may also be an agency who hires full-time employees.

This is not an actual "work at home business" but many prefer to not hire on permanently but to go from job to job. There is the possibility of some work being done remotely or at home. It can also become lucrative once you have worked for an agency for a while and they have good feedback on your work.

NOTE: Please refer to my websites for business resources, books, courses, software, equipment and supplies for the businesses in this book.   From time to time additional business opportunities will be posted on my website. I hope this information makes the research for your new business easier. Clicking on the links in the websites will take you to resources for each item.

http://www.pdsloss.com/
http://www.RealisticHomeBusinesses.com/

Chapter 7

Telecommuting--Employed Full or Part Time By One Company

Working remotely is a dream for many, but it is not for everyone. You probably already know the benefits of telecommuting, but consider the disadvantages as well. You must have self-motivation and not mind being somewhat isolated while working. The advantages and disadvantages are the same as those outlined in Chapter 3.

Popular Telecommuting Sectors

The following industries are the most likely candidates for telecommuting opportunities.

- Business Services
- Consumer Products, Retail, Manufacturing
- Financial Services
- Government/Defense & Space
- Healthcare, Pharmaceuticals
- Media/Publishing
- Technology & Telecommunications
- Travel

The federal government is one of the biggest supporters of telecommuting. There is even a law that requires all eligible employees in federal agencies to be allowed to telecommute.

Other legislation like the Clean Air Act and Americans with Disabilities Act have also supported the case for telecommuting.

Employer Telecommuting Benefits

The most forward thinking employers understand that telecommuting is not just a perk for the employee but also beneficial to the company. Employer benefits are listed here in case you should need reasons to win your case to work at home with an employer.

1. Save office space and reduce costs
Companies can save thousands on office space and parking for each employee that works remotely. The estimated cost of office space is $10,000 a year for the average employee.

2. Increases employee productivity and work/life balance
Studies show 15%-45% gains in productivity when employees work from home. Employees become more productive when they telecommute since there are fewer distractions, minimal (if any) socializing, and less stress.

3. Reduce absenteeism and help maintain operations
Telecommuters can work in bad weather, when children are home sick or during school closings, and in other instances where regular employees might instead take a personal or sick day. Reducing absenteeism can save large employers over $1 million per year. Telecommuting programs also enable both large and small companies to maintain their operations during times of emergency, severe weather events, or when there are concerns over health epidemics (e.g., flu outbreaks).

4. Increase employee retention and help attract new staff
Happier employees are usually better employees, and telecommuting definitely increases employee job satisfaction and loyalty. Telecommuting programs also help companies retain employees with circumstances such as needing to care for sick

family members, starting a new family, or needing to relocate for personal reasons. Reducing employee turnover saves on recruiting costs. Telecommuting is also an excellent incentive when looking for additional skilled staff in occupations that are high in demand. One third of CFOs in one survey said that a telecommuting program was the best way to attract top talent.

5. Help save the environment by eliminating commuting time
Fewer commuters mean fewer cars on the road, which translates to less air pollution and reduced fuel consumption. Telecommuting benefits everyone.

Telecommuting Friendly Companies

The following list of companies are telecommute friendly. This does not mean they have telecommuting jobs open so do not email a resume unless the company has an opening. Use the company website listed to see if there are jobs available and follow instructions for applying for any job listed. The decision to allow telecommuting is made between the manager and an employee and it has to be feasible to do the job by telecommuting. I suggest that you use this list to search for a job. Apply for listed jobs that you are interested in and qualified for and indicate that you are interested in telecommuting on your resume.

1-800 Contacts - https://jobs.1800contracts.com
1800Flowers.com - http://ww22.1800flowers.com
2 Places At 1 Time - http://www.2places.com/employment
3Com - http://www.3com.com
AAA Renewals - http://www.aaarenewals.com
Accenture - http://www.accenture.com
Aetna Life Insurance - http://www.aetna.com
AG Communication - http://www.ages.com
Air Products and Chemicals, Inc. - http://www.airproducts.com
American Airlines - http://www.aa.com
American Express - http://www.americanexpress.com
American Fidelity Assurance Company -
http://www.afadvantage.com

Ameritech - http://www.ameritech.com
Allergan - http://www.allergan.com
Allstate Insurance - http://www.allstate.com
Apple Computer - http://www.apple.com
Art & Logic - http://www.artlogic.com
Arthur Andersen Consulting - http://www.arthuranderson.com
AT&T - http://www.att.com/hr/
Bank of America - http://www.bofa.com/batoday/batoday.html
Banker's Trust - http://www.bankerstrust.com
Baxter Healthcare - http://www.baxter.com
Bell Atlantic - http://www.bellatlantic.com
Beneficial Corporation - http://www.beneficial.com
Bergen Brunswig - http://www.amerisourcebergen.com
Berlitz Translation Services - http://www.berlitz.com
Blue Cross/Blue Shield - http://www.bcbs.com
Blue Cross/Blue Shield of Maryland - http://www.bluecross.com
Brocade Communications Systems - http://www.brocade.com
CFW Communications - http://www.cfw.com
Chevron - http://www.chevron.com
Cigna - http://www.cigna.com
Cincinnati Bell - http://www.cinbelltel.com
CISCO Systems, Inc. - http://www.cisco.com
Citibank - http://www.citibank.com
Compaq - http://www.compaq.com
Computer Curriculum Corp. - http://www.cccnet.com
Connext Inc. - http://www.connext.com
Creative Freelance - http://www.freelancers.com
Creative Labs - http://www.soundblaster.com
Dell Computer - http://www.dell.com
Deloitte - http://www.deloitte.com
Detroit Free Press - Blue Cross/Blue Shield -
http://www.bcbs.comfreep.com
Diamond Multimedia Systems, Inc. - http://www.diamondmm.com
Digital Equipment Corporation - http://www.digital.com
Digital News - http://www.digitalnews.com
DSP Technology, Inc. - http://www.dspt.com
Dun & Bradstreet - http://www.dnb.com
DuPont - http://www.dupont.com
Ernest & Young, L.L.P. - http://www.ey.com

Eastman Kodak Company - http://www.kodak.com
Edify Corp. - http://www.edify.com
En Pointe Technologies - http://www.enpointe.com
Equitable Life Assurance - http://www.equitable.com
Fannie Mae - http://www.fanniemae.com
Federal Express - http://www.fedex.com
Gannett - http://www.gannett.com
Geico - http://www.geico.com
General Electic Nuclear Energy - http://www.ge.com
Government Jobs - http://www.careersingovernment.com
GTE - http://www.gte.com
Healthnet - http://www.healthnet.com
Hewlett-Packard - http://www.hp.com
Honeywell - http://www.honeywell.com
Hughes Aircraft - http://www.hughes.com
Hypermedia Group, Inc. - http://www.hmg.com
IBM - http://www.ibm.com
Implicit Inc. - http://www.implicitweb.com
Initial Call - http://www.initialcall.com
Inktomi Corp. - http://www.inktomi.com
Insignia Solutions, Inc. - http://www.insignia.com
Intel - http://www.intel.com
Intracorp - http://www.intracorp.com
JCPenney - http://www.jcpenney.com
John Hancock Insurance - http://www.johnhancock.com
Knight-Ridder Information, Inc. - http://www.krinfo.com
LAM Research Corp. - http://www.lamrc.com
Lanier Business Products - http://www.lanier.com
Lawrence Livermore National Laboratory - http://www.llnl.gov
LINK Resources Corporation - http://www.linkresources.com
Los Angeles Times – http://www.latimes.com
Lumisys, Inc. - http://www.lumisys.com
Macromedia Inc. - http://www.macromedia.com
MacWEEK - http://www.zdnet.com
Maxtor Corp. - http://www.maxtor.com
MCI - http://www.mci.com
McGraw Hill - http://www.mcgraw-hill.com
Meridian Data, Inc. - http://www.meridian-data.com
Microsoft - http://www.microsoft.com

Molecular Devices Corp. - http://www.moldev.com
National Association of Insurance Commissioners - http://www.naic.com
NEC Electronics, Inc. - http://www.nec.com
NetApp - http://www.netapp.com
Netframe Systems, Inc. - http://www.netframe.com
Netscape Communications Corp. - http://www.netframe.com
New York Life Insurance Company - http://www.newyorklife.com
NewsBank - http://www.newsbank.com/
Newsbytes News Service - http://www.newsbytes.com
Nike - http://www.nike.com
Nortel (Northern Telecom) - http://www.nortel.com
Oak Technology, Inc. - http://www.oaktech.com
Octel Communications Corp. - http://www.octel.com
Optimized Cable Company - http://www.optimization-world.com
Oracle Corp. - http://www.oracle.com
Orange County Register - http://www.ocregister.com
Pacific Bell - http://www.sbc.com
PC Week - http://www.zdnet.com
Peoplesoft, Inc. - http://www.peoplesoft.com
Philips C&P Division - http://www.philips.com
PricewaterhouseCoopers - http://www.pwc.com
Proxim - http://www.proxim.com/about/careers/index.html
Quantum Corp. - http://www.quantum.com
Quintus Corp. - http://www.quintus.com
Radius, Inc. - http://www.radius.com
RAND Corporation - http://www.rand.org
Raytheon Systems - http://www.raytheon.com/rsc
Remedy Corp. - http://www.remedy.com
S. C. Johnson & Son - http://www.scjohnson.com
Santa Cruz Operation, Inc. - http://www.sco.com
Sears, Roebuck & Co. - http://www.sears.com
Share Data, Inc. - http://www.sharedata.com
Shared Technologies - http://www.sharedtechnologies.com
Siemens Business Communication Systems, Inc. - http://www.siemens.com
Sprint - http://www.sprint.com
St. Paul Travelers - http://www.stpaultravelers.com
Sun Microsystems - http://www.sun.com

Symantec Corp. - http://www.symantec.com
Tab Products Co. - http://www.tabproducts.com
Tandem Computers, Inc. - http://www.tandem.com
Telcom Semiconductor, Inc. - http://www.telcom-semi.com
Texas Instruments - http://www.ti.com
The Seattle Times - http://www.seattletimes.nwsource.com
Time, Inc. - http://www.timeinc.com
Travelers Corporation - http://www.travelers.com
UMI/Data Courier - http://www.umi.com
Unigroup Inc. - http://www.unigroup.com
United Press International - http://www.upi.com
US West Communications - http://www.uswest.com
VirtualStaff - h http://www.virtualstaff.com
Verifone, Inc. - http://www.verifone.com
W. W. Norton & Company - http://www.wwnorton.com
Wendy's - http://www.wendys.com
Weyerhauser - http://www.weyerhauser.com
Xerox - http://www.xerox.com
Xyratex - http://www.xyratex.com
Zitel Corp. - http://www.zitel.com

NOTE: Please refer to my websites for business resources, books, courses, software, equipment and supplies for the businesses in this book. From time to time additional business opportunities will be posted on my website. I hope this information makes the research for your new business easier. Clicking on the links in the websites will take you to resources for each item.

http://www.pdsloss.com/
http://www.RealisticHomeBusinesses.com/

Chapter 8

Home Office Professions

This chapter lists professions you can do from your home office. Some require travel and others require only initial or periodic meetings with clients but the work is done in your home office. Online freelance work is discussed in chapter 9 since there are numerous opportunities that are easier to describe together.

Bookkeeping & Payroll

Bookkeepers are in strong demand. Every business needs some form of bookkeeping whether it is a one-person operation or the business has thousands of employees. You should have a background and knowledge of bookkeeping and enjoy working with numbers. This is a great part-time business you can do anytime. You can build a part-time business while working full-time at another job.

Skills

Unlike accountants, bookkeepers do not need a professional license. You can become certified by the American Institute of Professional Bookkeepers (www.aipb.com). Certification is not necessary but it adds to your list of qualifications. There are a number of bookkeeping classes online and offered at local colleges.

http;//www.pdsloss.com

Equipment

A bookkeeping business is inexpensive to start. You will need the equipment and software on the following list. The most popular bookkeeping software packages are QuickBooks Pro and Peachtree.

- Computer
- Printer
- Phone
- Fax
- Word Processing Software
- Bookkeeping Software
- Calculator
- Shredder

A small space in your home is all that is needed. Make sure you have a separate area in your home if you will have to meet with clients. There will be no zoning issues since it would be seldom that a client will come to your office.

Income

Bookkeepers can expect to earn $20 to $75 an hour. The average client billing will be $300 per month and will require six to eight hours a month to complete. Typically your fee should be a standard monthly charge. Charging by the hour is an administrative headache and selling services is easier when your new client knows what to expect. Be sure to have a letter agreement outlining specific services that will be provided and circumstances or additional services for which additional fees will be charged. Your fee will be dependent on the complexity and size of the business and number of employees.

If you have experience in one industry you may want to specialize by seeking bookkeeping clients within that industry. For instance, if you have worked in a medical practice most of your life, you could send a letter and brochure to all the medical facilities in your area

42

stating that your expertise would be an asset to the efficiency of their business. Other specialty areas include: law firms, restaurants, bars, retail stores, automotive companies, construction firms or any businesses in your area. To avoid being overwhelmed, start with businesses that have three to twenty employees. This is a comfortable size and will keep the task manageable while you are gaining experience. Focus on small businesses that cannot afford to have a bookkeeper on staff full time and are too busy doing their business to do the bookkeeping themselves.

You will be entrusted with private company and confidential employee information. Maintaining a private and secure office is essential. Others should not have access to the computer or office that you are using to do books or payroll. If you are doing payroll, you will have a number of individuals social security information. Use a shredder before disposing of sensitive information.

Get a business name through your state. An EIN (Employer Identification Number) described in Chapter 15 will protect your social security number since you will have multiple clients. Join the local Chamber of Commerce and/or Better Business Bureau. Create business cards, post cards and tri-fold brochures. A good advertising strategy is to send a brochure or postcard to all of the DBA filings printed in your local paper. Watch for advertisements for a part-time bookkeeper and send your brochure with a cover letter. Hand out your brochures and business cards walking door to door in industrial areas with small spaces. Create a website to mirror your brochure and add more information to sell your business. A website helps you gain the trust of your customer by giving you more of a business presence than a brochure or card. Customers want to know something about the company and the people in charge of the company.

Business Plan Writer

Writing a good business plan is essential to starting a business. Many new small businesses have started recently out of necessity.

Layoffs and large business failures have created opportunities for newly unemployed people to start their own businesses. New businesses should always create a business plan to see if their new business is a viable idea before investing money and time. A business plan will be required if a loan is needed.

As a business plan writer, you will take the hopes and dreams of would be entrepreneurs and translate their data, facts, and figures into a written report. Without a solid business plan, financial assistance cannot be sought. There is a good opportunity for business plan writers and they may also want to branch out into related services of grant writing and resume writing. Every business should have a business plan, regardless of financing needs. A business plan can show what steps must be completed for a business to be profitable. Sometimes the business plan will show that the business is not feasible which might save your client a large amount of money and time.

Skills

A background in business finance, accounting or business development is helpful in starting this type of business. The business owner will rely on you to take his ideas and dreams and to develop a solid plan. A sample outline is provided below.

Business Plan Outline
- Business Profile
- The Vision and People
- Communications
- Organization
- Licenses, Permits, and Business Names
- Insurance
- Premises
- Accounting & Cash Flow
- Financing
- E-Commerce

- Acquisitions
- Marketing
- Financial Attachments

There is a large amount of information included under each heading. After the plan is finished, the client should know how much money is needed for startup, money needed to run the business every month, and a breakdown of where the money will be spent. Next would be how much money they expect to make and how long is estimated until the break-even point or profit made.

As you can see, business plans are very tedious and thorough. You must have the ability to pay great attention to detail and work well with numbers. There is some good software with templates available to help you format information easily. Don't shortchange yourself on the amount you charge for this service, since business plans are very time consuming. Your client may also have tight deadlines if their plan is needed for financing for their business.

Equipment

You will need the equipment and software listed below. Business Plan writing requires a minimum of startup expenses. You will need an Internet connection to transfer documents back and forth to your clients. There are a number of good business plan books and software that can make your job much easier and do all of the formatting for you.

- Computer
- Printer
- Phone
- Fax
- Word Processing Software
- Business Plan Software

Income

The recent price of a professionally written business plan is from $399 to $7500 for an involved business plan. This can be a very lucrative business. Advertise by making flyers, business cards, postcards, a website, or newspaper ads. Your website is your online brochure, resume, and sales letter. Join business associations since new businesses will gather at some of the meetings.

Copywriter

There are a number of opportunities for someone who can write well. The main goal in copywriting is to sell. Copywriting is found everywhere, on the Internet, direct mail, television, radio, brochures, and more. All of these mediums require a copywriter and the sales depend on the quality of writing in the copy.

Copywriting is a very rewarding and well paid field. You can expect some long days and tight deadlines but at other times set your own schedule. Traditional jobs for copywriters were with advertising agencies, magazines, newspapers, or public relations firms. With the advent of the Internet, it is now possible for a copywriter to work as a freelance writer. There will be no shortage of work if you are good at your craft.

Skills

A copywriter needs specific writing skills in the art of selling and persuasion. If you do not already have this skill, there are many good courses online, at colleges and sometimes self-taught. There are many good books on copywriting which you should read.

You can learn a lot from your junk mail and Internet sales pages. The ads you get in the mail are called "controls" which are part of the direct mail industry. Copywriters write this direct mail. Study your direct mail and online offers. Try changing the offer letter to make it better and more attractive without changing the prices. Study what part of the writing makes you want to buy the product or at least be interested.

Most copywriters have some sort of background in writing. You may have a degree in English, journalism or communications. Experience in marketing or advertising can be a huge help.

Equipment

You will need the equipment and software listed below. Copywriting requires a minimum of startup expenses. You will need an Internet connection to transfer documents back and forth to clients. There are a number of copywriting books you should own including reference materials like a dictionary and thesaurus.

- Computer
- Printer
- Phone
- Fax
- Word Processing Software

Prospective clients will want to see samples of your work. Build a portfolio by writing articles or sales letters for an imaginary product. When you complete several samples, build a website to market your services. Join your local Chamber of Commerce and network with local business people.

Make cold calls to local graphic designers or website developers. Occasionally, they need the services of a copywriter and you can leave business cards and brochures with them. There are online opportunities as well in chapter 9 of this book. Be careful with the freelance online sites that you do not underbid your services. If you do work for one of the freelance sites, be sure to do a good job and complete the work on time since your name and reputation will be tied to those services. Many clients will go to the freelance boards to see if you are listed and what your feedback was on assignments.

Income

The salary range for a copywriter is from $35 to $100 an hour. For those who specialize in a field like pharmaceutical writing, income will range from $70 to $100 per hour. Entry-level copywriters normally start at the lower end of the range until they get more experience and have a quality portfolio.

As a new freelance copywriter you may need to accept almost any job offer while proving your capabilities. Building a quality portfolio and list of clients is a priority.   Repeat business and word of mouth will increase and spread your business. Develop a price list for your writing specialties so your clients have an idea of what they will be charged and you won't forget your prices. An example of charges is: a 350 word web home page for $200 to $500 or a long sales letter for $1500. As you gain experience, you can increase your prices and you may want to specialize in one field.

Associations

Editorial Freelancers Association -- http://www.the-efa.org/
American Association of Advertising Agencies   --
http://www.aaaa.org/pages/default.aspx
American Marketing Association --
http://www.marketingpower.com/Pages/default.aspx
Association of National Advertisers -- http://www.ana.net/
Association of Professional Freelance Copywriters --
http://aopfc.com/index.html

Editing/Editorial Services

People make mistakes when it comes to writing. Many documents are important and cannot afford to contain mistakes. If you are writing a grant and use bad grammar or are too wordy it could mean the loss of grant money. The wrong words in training manuals could, for instance, cost a life if the subject was on electricity or medicine and the reader misunderstood the directions. Some people struggle with finding the right words, spelling or grammar. When someone has reviewed a paper or book multiple times they tend to consistently miss the same errors. Sometimes people are so "wordy" that whoever is reading loses interest and tosses the material.

Skills

You may have transferrable skills if you have worked in education, for corporations, or anywhere that editing was a job or a habit. If you find mistakes in publications or books that you are reading, this business may fit you well.

Freelance opportunities are expanding for editors due to the increasing numbers of self-published authors and new websites requiring new content. There are many other opportunities for editors and you may find one niche rather than offering multiple services.

Below is a list of the types of services you may want to provide:

- Advertising and Marketing
- Advertising Copy
- Annual Reports & Public Documents
- Books
- Business Plans
- Business Proposals & RFPs
- Business Solicitation Documents
- Catalogues, Brochures & Flyers
- Company Fact Sheets
- Consumer Product Manuals
- Corporate Communications
- Display Ads
- Executive Bios
- Founder and Partner Profiles
- Fundraising Letters
- Grant Proposals

- Indexing
- Internal Business Documents
- Market Research Surveys
- Marketing Proposals
- Media Kits
- Newsletters, E-zines & Blogs
- Policies and Procedures Manuals
- Press Releases
- Programming Manuals
- Promotional Materials
- Prospectuses
- Publicity & Public Relations Materials
- Query Letters
- Reference Guides
- Sales and Promotional Letters
- Speeches
- Teaching and Training Manuals

Equipment

You will need the equipment and software listed below. Editing requires a minimum of startup expenses.   An Internet connection is required to transfer documents back and forth to your clients.

- Computer
- Printer
- Phone
- Fax
- Word Processing Software

Even the best editors need reference materials like a dictionary, thesaurus, or style guide.   Purchase several good editing books for your reference. There are a number of online courses on editing, proofreading, and indexing. These courses are offered by local colleges as well.

You can work from virtually anywhere. You could edit a book out of an RV while you were traveling. If you advertise for local editing, you can work out of your home office. A small space is all that is needed. There will be no zoning issues since it would be seldom that a client would come to your office.

Income

Recent Rates are from $20 to $100 an hour and indexing is $3 to $12 a page.   You can do a search on the Internet to find out what other editing businesses charge for different services.

Decide which services to provide and pricing for each service. Make a list of editing services and prices to be consistent when quoting your fees to different clients. Your price may change if one is a much more complex job. Make your editing business fit your skills and your personality.

When someone describes a project, they want a price per hour or for the job. Each service should have a set price, unless the project described has too many variables. Editors charge by the hour, project, page, or word. Clients usually prefer flat rate pricing. You could get burned quoting a project price in the beginning. With experience you will be able to quote an accurate flat rate fee. A letter or contract agreement should be signed by both parties so they know what to expect for a flat fee and what services involve additional fees. Working by the hour requires keeping accurate records of hours worked to substantiate the client's bill. You can also bid on work for a freelance company as described in Chapter 9 of this book.

Advertise by making flyers, business cards, postcards, a website, or newspaper ads. Your website is your online brochure, resume, and sales letter. You may also want a price list on your website. Contact publishing companies in writing. Describe what services you can perform for them, relating the services to what they publish. Follow up by phone. Target writer's groups or conferences. Hang flyers on university bulletin boards and coffee shops where writers or students frequent. Leave business cards at any businesses you visit. Finish assignments on time and deliver what you promise. Word of mouth is a great advertisement for this business. Freelance ratings are important if you work for a business like Elance.

Organizations

- American Copy Editors Society-- http://www.copydesk.org/
- American Society of Indexers— www.asindexing.org
- Editorial Freelancers Association-- www.the-efa.org
- Editorium.com-- www.editorium.com

Event Planner

The event planning field is a multi-billion dollar industry. You can work out of your home with no employees and a small office, large enough to be able to plan and keep track of events you are setting up for clients. The startup costs are low, and your business can be run without any full-time employees. All it takes is organization skills and a degree of creativity. Have you ever planned or help plan a class or large family reunion? If so, you probably already have many of the skills needed.

Individuals and companies often find they lack the time and expertise to plan events themselves. Independent event planners can relieve the stress by stepping in and giving special events the attention they deserve.

Events you may be hired to plan:
- Celebrations (weddings, private parties, fairs, parades, reunions, birthdays, anniversaries)
- Education (conferences, meetings, graduations)
- Promotions (grand openings, product launches, political rallies, fashion shows, fundraisers)

Skills

Below are some of the skills and tasks you will be required to accomplish. You may have to handle all or some part of these tasks. Tasks will depend on the size and type of the event.

- Conducting research
- Creating an event design
- Finding a site
- Arranging for food, decor and entertainment
- Planning transportation to and from the event
- Sending invitations to attendees
- Arranging any necessary accommodations for attendees
- Coordinating the activities of event personnel
- Supervising at the site
- Conducting evaluations of the event

Hands-on experience is needed for the event planning business. If you have no current skills, apply for a job working with an existing event planning business to acquire experience. If need be, take on a voluntary role. Start making contacts in the industry and begin to learn the tips of the trade. You do not need to be "certified" to start a career in event planning. Most event planning certifications require at least three to five years of experience before taking the certification test. Event planning certification is a measure of what you already know about the industry. It certifies that you do know the field and you are an expert. When you become certified, if you choose to do so, it is a designation you can put after your name and on your brochure and website to show your expertise.

You do need to learn the basics and get some hands-on experience. Learn everything you can about event planning, volunteer or work for someone for a short time and network.

Equipment

The following list of equipment is needed to help with research and planning. You need to be able to type agreements for your services and print or email bills.

- Computer
- Printer
- Phone
- Fax
- Word Processing Software
- Internet Connection

Consider buying insurance for your event planning business. You want to be covered in case the worst possible thing happens and someone sues you.

Set up a website listing events you are willing to plan. List previous events, expertise, relevant experience, degrees, certificates, and any other information significant to your business. Your website is your online resume, portfolio, and sales letter. Design your business cards and brochures and have them professionally printed.

Market your event planning business. Join the local Chamber of Commerce and/or Better Business Bureau. Create business cards, post cards, and tri-fold brochures. Put ads in your local paper, Craig's List, and local magazines.

Income

The average income for an event planner in the United States ranges from $46,000 to $64,000 a year. Event planners who handle events such as movie premieres, weddings, trade shows and banquets often receive tips. The standard gratuity is 15 to 20 percent of the cost of the service. Tips are warranted considering the long hours and weekends that event planners work. It may take 80 to 175 hours for an event planner and staff to produce an important event.

To make a living as a successful event planner, go where the money is. Once you are a competent planner, look for these areas of event planning: large scale events, corporate meetings, corporate events, and corporative incentive trips. You can do smaller events in-between but without the larger events, making a living may be a problem.

Associations

Event Planners Association (EPA) --
http://eventplannersassociation.com/
Meeting Professionals International (MPI) --
http://www.mpiweb.org/Home

Grant Writer

If you have good writing skills, can follow directions, and enjoy helping nonprofits, you may want to start a grant writing consultant business. Skilled grant writers are in demand by not only the people you would think of as nonprofits, but also schools, fire departments, and sheriff departments.   Every nonprofit organization needs a grant writer. Many hire consultants and others hire full-time grant writers.

The majority of grants are given to organizations that have nonprofit status also known as 501(c)(3) status. These organizations help their communities at the local, national or international level. The majority of nonprofits do not have a grant writer on staff. There are not a lot of skilled grant writers for them to choose from.

Skills

To become a professional grant writer, you need skills in writing, storytelling, consulting, research, program planning, evaluation, interviewing, public relations, internet marketing, and budgeting. You may be hired to research the availability of grants for a specific nonprofit organization. Finding the sources quickly is important for not only available grants, but statistics. It is imperative to take a class or at a minimum read books on grant writing to understand the jargon and participants.

Good speaking skills are necessary to first sell yourself as the grant writer who should be hired and next to present your ideas on the direction the grant should follow. You may be hired to do research, present your findings, set up a year's schedule, write the grants, and then prepare follow up reports during and after the grant funding.

Some grants are 50 pages long. The grant funders all have their specific rules that must be followed. If the grant specifications state the grant must be formatted in 12 point type with one inch margins, that is how the grant must be formatted, without exception. Funders question an organization's ability to manage the money they are awarded if they cannot follow simple formatting directions. As a representative of the nonprofit organization you must have credibility and integrity. All information about the grant and your client must remain confidential. Grant writing is a specialized skill that needs to be practiced.

Refuse to work for anyone who you know has intentions of misusing the grant funds. Some grants allow payments for grant writers to be made from grant funds, while others do not.

Equipment

The following list of equipment is needed for grant research and preparing and submitting grants. Equipment is also needed to prepare agreements for your services and print or email bills. Some grants will be written on your word processor and then transferred to an online form for submission. Subscriptions to several data bases may be required to research grant availability. Much of your research will be done online.

- Computer
- Printer
- Phone
- Fax
- Word Processing Software
- Internet Connection
- Funding Data Bases
- Reference Books

There are a number of good books and courses on grant writing. You can find well-written samples of funded grants online that are advantageous to study.

Income

A grant writer can expect to make an annual income from $50,000 to $300,000. The income potential depends on a variety of factors. Hourly rates start at $25 and go up to $150. The average grant writer with a few years experience and a good track record of receiving grants will charge $70 per hour dependent on location. Higher rates are charged in larger cities. Some grant writers charge by the project. Fees depend on the length and complexity of the grant document. Consulting firms charge a daily rate between $500 and $2,000.

A signed contract by both you and the organization is necessary to clarify terms. Payment is normally paid in full prior to the grant or research work being done if the total is $500 or less. When your fee is higher than $500, require a preliminary payment of 50 percent down with the balance due on completion and delivery of the grant. Do not start work until the contract is signed and you have the payment spelled out in the contract.

A grant writer must accept that their efforts may not be successful in receiving every grant written. Your client must also understand that there is a lot of competition. There are a number of factors determining who receives the grant. Sometimes a grant is awarded to someone the funder knows. Geography factors for the areas that funders want to include will come into play. If they gave money for something very similar to your cause recently and need to spread the money around, the grant will be given to someone else. Many other factors come into play which have nothing to do with how the grant was written.

Associations

Listed below are the websites of some of the databases and grant writer associations. The associations have a lot to offer with everything from training to insurance.

Foundation Center -- http://www.foundationcenter.org/ (database)
Grant Gopher -- www.grantgopher.com (database)
Pen American Center -- http://www.pen.org/ (database)
American Grant Writers Association -- http://www.agwa.us/ (association)
Grant Professionals Association -- http://grantprofessionals.org/ (association)

Teaching Online

Over 80% of learners today have taken at least one online course and that number is expected to increase to 100% in the next few years. To keep up with the demand for online courses, universities are turning to part-time teachers and other educational businesses are looking for people to either teach online classes or develop video courses on DVDs. Prepare for this job by taking online courses in areas you teach or want to teach. Note how the course is structured. Note the cost of an online course with instructor vs. written material, how are assignments given, and how are tests structured and taken. Is the result for the student a college credit, certificate or knowledge. Writers, editors, illustrators, actors, animators, instructors, programmers and dozens of other professionals work in online training jobs. Online classes use many kinds of resources and skills to teach many kinds of students.

Skills

Some courses taught online are instructor-led. This means the instructor makes assignments, returns grades, gives tests, answers questions and even delivers live lectures via the Internet. Instructors often get to know each student in their class, which makes online courses a little more like tutoring than traditional classroom instruction.

Some courses, taught online, are not instructor-led. Instructors work with writers, editors, animators and video professionals to create a standalone instructional course that delivers some type of skill. This course may be given on the Internet or on a DVD. They may also include printable lessons or illustrations and sometimes a test.

Equipment

The following list of equipment is needed for online teaching. A small space in your home is all that is needed and possibly a place to video your class. There will be no zoning issues since it would be seldom that a student would come to your home.

- Computer
- Large Monitor
- Printer
- Phone
- Fax

- Word Processing Software
- Internet Connection
- Backup Hard Drive
- Video Software
- Video Equipment

Income

The average salary for teaching an online class depends on the kind of class you are teaching, your degrees and experience and whether or not you are teaching with an institution. There are a variety of online teaching positions, from private teaching and tutoring to professorships at online colleges and universities. Salaries range from $56,000 to $86,000. If you produce a unique online class or DVD, you may make considerably more with ongoing sets of courses.

Associations

National Education Association (NEA) --
http://www.nea.org/home/30103.htm
WizIQ Education Online --
http://www.wiziq.com/teachers/associations/page2
World Association for Online Education -- http://waoe.org/

Degree Associated Teaching

Some of these opportunities would be directly for universities and colleges developing and teaching their online courses for credits to receive degrees. Teaching degree courses for credit would most likely require a degree and teaching experience. Other opportunities not requiring a degree would be courses teaching a subject, not for credits but for certification or information. I have personally taken numerous online classes. Some of these were through Universities and colleges and others were to learn a specific skill.

The demand for online teachers is growing at a staggering rate since the Internet been integrated into almost everyone's life. Many working people want to take classes but find commuting difficult. For some the cost of fuel commuting to school is an issue. Being able to take classes on their time schedule may make the difference in someone being able to get a degree or learn a skill.

In my own career, I remember trying to finish my degree while working. What a pain to have the class I needed only be available during the day. I had to get special permission at work to take off to get to class and then work extra hours into the evening to make up the missed time. Later I took night classes. After a hard day at work, driving miles to attend night school to take classes was tiresome. It was also expensive due to commuting since I lived in the country. The classes I have taken online have been a joy.

This industry is taking off due to the Internet and the opportunity for schools and universities to make far more income by offering classes online. Many people do not have time or their location limits availability to regular school classes. This field is growing exponentially.

Below is a list of places to consider for teaching for online. I have personally taken numerous classes through Ed to Go, Lynda, Interweave Press, Nightingale Conant, and many others. I have taken grant writing, nonprofit management, photography, and many software classes.

- Many Local Universities or colleges
- Ed to Go
- Lynda
- University of Phoenix
- Walden
- Capella
- Kaplan University
- University of Maryland

- Devry

Find more opportunities by searching online. Here are some searches you can try: online tutor, online instructor, instructor + work from home, online + professor, online + tutor, and many more combinations. This field is expanding and if you have the right credentials, you will have a good chance of finding work.

Non Degree Teaching

If you do not have a degree, there are many other opportunities teaching online. Do you have a niche talent? Say, you like model trains and want to put together a DVD or online class to teach someone how to build the small buildings to scale that are used in the model railroad hobby. Maybe you tool leather or braid leather and want to teach others how to do this craft. Niche photography classes are popular. You might be a product photographer and be able to teach others how to take pictures for marketing purposes. Baby boomers are retiring or nearing retirement and want to pursue activities they never had time to do while they were working.

There are many niche DVD courses on jewelry making, enameling, Native American beading, weaving, spinning, patinas, cold connections for metal, metalsmithing, silversmithing, soldering, colored pencils, polymer clay techniques, quilt making, sewing, engraving, photography, stock and option trading, forex trading, dancing, exercise programs, and more.

Teach about your niche locally or make a DVD. Find your strongest skills and think of the training class you could produce. Purchase a course in either your niche or something similar and pay attention to how the class is organized. Is the course organized in an easy to understand manner? Does this look like a professional video or could you improve on an aspect of the production or quality? A new business can come from teaching almost any craft and is certainly more lucrative than doing the craft yourself. When you become the expert by furnishing a DVD or eBook, then you could also sell items to do the craft and put together a very lucrative business. I have seen many people become a huge success with this. Some of them even operate out of their RV while going south for the winter. Think about your own website with educational DVDs or eBooks and the materials or a package of materials needed for the craft you teach.

Tutoring Business

Tutoring children or adults can be a lucrative endeavor. You must have the proper background and/or education for the type of tutoring you want to start. This business is virtually recession-proof and is a growing industry. The startup investment is minimal and advertising costs are inexpensive. Time must be spent in the beginning by marketing your services.

Start by talking to local schools. Leave your cards and brochures with the guidance counselors. You can also post an ad in the local newspapers. Place posters, flyers or business cards in places in your local community where potential customers frequent. Ideas would be: community centers, schools, church, laundromats, or stores that have a bulletin board that will allow your materials. After you have been a tutor for a while, word of mouth will contribute to expanding your business.

Requirements

The only requirement for this business is that you know your subject and know how to teach.

Income

The expected income from tutoring is $50 an hour and in some areas more. Tutoring special needs children could bring in considerably more per hour.

Associations

National Tutoring Association -- http://ntatutor.com/
Association for the Tutoring Profession -- http://www.myatp.org/

Insurance/Insurance Related Services

An insurance agent assists individuals, families and corporations in selecting and purchasing the best insurance policy that will protect their lifestyles, health and/or property. Job requirements will differ slightly depending on the type of insurance sold. For example, a health insurance agent sells insurance policies that cover medical and dental care, while life insurance agents specialize in selling beneficiary polices, which may be used for educational funding and retirement income annuities.

Skills

A variety of skills are necessary to be a successful insurance agent. Insurance agents need to be self-motivated and have initiative in order to acquire potential clients. This field is highly competitive in nature. Efficient time management skills are necessary because you will be responsible for handling the insurance needs of many clients during their work day. Insurance agents should possess good verbal and written communication skills in order to explain essential information regarding insurance policies, as well as prepare and maintain client records. Confidence is another important skill insurance agents need to possess, since they spend much of their time trying to convince potential clientele to purchase insurance and/or financial services.

Every state requires insurance agents to be licensed.   Separate licenses are required to sell life and health insurance or property and casualty insurance. Most states require pre-licensing courses and passing state examinations. After becoming licensed, most state licensing authorities require insurance agents to continue their education by attending classes on subjects such as insurance laws and consumer protection every two years.

You may want to first work directly for an insurance company in order to get the necessary experience to go out on your own and become an independent insurance agent. Many insurance companies prefer to hire insurance agents with a college degree in business, finance or economics. Newly hired insurance agents normally receive on-the-job training from experienced co-workers, allowing them to learn how to successfully conduct business interactions with clients.

Independent insurance agents or brokers, many of whom represent a variety of companies, are responsible for finding the best insurance rates and policies for all of their clientele along with investigating pending insurance claims. Although they are often referred to as "independent insurance agents", individuals who provide insurance-related services must still meet each of the legal requirements of an independent contractor if you want to have your own business and not be considered an employee of one company. You may still work out of your home office when you work for one company. You would be considered an employee, but would still have some home office deductions while having the freedom of working from your home office.

Critical to the determination of whether you are self employed is that you remain free from direction and control over both the means and the manner by which services are provided. While some brokers may be able to provide their clients with products from a number of different insurers, many insurance workers are contractually obligated to only offer one provider's products. To be considered as self employed, you must be free to set prices, vary the product line, or negotiate the basis for their compensation from the insurer.

Equipment

The following list of equipment is needed for an insurance business. A small space in your home is all that is needed. If you meet with clients in your home office, a separate entrance to the office is a good idea with a dedicated bathroom.

- Computer
- Printer
- Phone
- Fax
- Word Processing Software
- Internet Connection
- Backup Hard Drive

Income

Insurance agents earn from $30,000 to $115,000. Income depends on experience and whether or not you are actually an "independent agent."

Graphic Designer/Illustrator

Graphic designers create effective visual designs for websites, business cards, brochures, letterheads, posters, billboards, presentations, television, movies and other marketing materials. Graphic designs make websites and other visual presentations stand out and get attention.

Skills

Become proficient using graphic design software. Courses are available online and at local colleges to train you in graphics design. It is important to posses the proper expertise in this field to have a successful graphic design business. Be familiar with the use of some of the more popular software, such as Illustrator or InDesign by Adobe.

Equipment

The following list of equipment is needed for a graphic design business. You will need a high-end computer with a good graphics card, large monitor, backup hard drive, printer, phone, fax, and graphic design software. A small space in your home is all that is needed. The best space would have good natural light since you are dealing with designs and colors. There will be no zoning issues since it would be seldom that a client would come to your office.

- Computer
- Large Monitor
- Printer
- Phone
- Fax
- Word Processing Software
- Internet Connection
- Backup Hard Drive
- Graphics Design Software

Set up a website showcasing your best work, expertise, relevant experience, degrees and any other information significant to your business. Your website is your online resume, portfolio, and sales letter. Prospective clients expect that your materials are going to look polished and professional. Design your business cards and brochures and have them professionally printed. Create a portfolio of your best work for potential clients.

Market your graphic design business. Join the local Chamber of Commerce and/or Better Business Bureau. Look for companies who are not large enough to hire a full-time graphic designer. Commercial and high-end real estate offices use graphic designers for their marketing products and websites. Put ads in your local paper, Craig's List, and local magazines. Website designers are also in need of high-end graphics. Smaller advertising agencies that cannot afford a full-time designer might use your services. Electronics firms need designers for marketing brochures and manuals. See Chapter 9, Freelance Marketplace, for short-term graphics designer/illustrator gigs.

Start a graphic design blog, where you can display your graphic design talent. By creating a blog and driving traffic to your graphic design blog you are cultivating trust for the viewers. Blogs have become very popular over the past few years and taking advantage of its popularity is free advertising for your graphic design business.

Keep your blog up-to-date. In order to rank high on Google search engine it is vital to keep your blog entries current and interesting to the viewers, this is a great way to be sure to continue to draw more traffic to your site which translates into more potential customers.

Income

Graphic designers earn an average of $39,900 per year, with very experienced designers making $98,600 yearly. Income is tied to the level of skill and experience of the designer.

Landman—Oil and Gas

The oil and gas business is going through a major transformation. Oil prices seem to rise almost daily, compared to the major decline for the last 20 years. Since the business was declining and it was thought you could not make a good living, people entering the business have also been in steady decline. Companies are now scrambling to hire experienced people but there are not enough available. The demand for experienced oil and gas workers of all kinds is skyrocketing.

Since there is a shortage of workers, companies pay landmen a good wage. The time to enter this field is now since in the future there may be license and training requirements. By entering now, you would more than likely be grandfathered in if a license is required at a later date.

Before an oil or gas well can be drilled, the mineral rights must be leased. It is the landman's job to research the mineral rights and negotiate a lease with the mineral right owners. A surface rights agreement has to be negotiated with the property owners before drilling. The property owner may not necessarily own the mineral rights, or they may own a percentage of the rights. The landman negotiates an upfront lease payment and the royalty that will be paid if oil or gas is found. A landman must be detail oriented since even a minor error in a contract could cost millions of dollars. You will work for an oil company or a leasing company to acquire leases.

Skills

To be an oil and gas landman, you need to learn the processes involved in determining ownership of surface owners of land, mineral rights, locating heirs, determining what percentage that people own, and finding owners or their heirs. Learning and understanding the contract involved in leasing mineral rights is paramount since mistakes can cost a company large sums of money. A landman should be people oriented and able to develop a comfortable rapport. You will be trying to convince people to lease their mineral rights to your company. This will require that you research the going rate for leases in the area and the company you work for may give you some leeway on the rates you offer. Of course you will be trying to get the best rates for your company.

There are two types of landmen. One works directly for a company and the other is independent, working for themselves on a consulting contract basis. The money you can make from this profession is substantially higher than most professions that require considerably more training. Many landmen make $400 to $500 a day and that does not include payments for hotels, meals and auto expenses.

Landman have a lot of freedom. Most of the time you can work out of your home and travel to courthouses and towns nearby without having to commute to an office. You may also have to travel and stay in a hotel on jobs which are too far from home to commute easily for courthouse research and to deal with land and mineral right owners. The company you work for will normally pay all expenses related to the job which includes hotels, car rental and meals. An area may be booming, which could require your physical presence for several months.

You may need to be physically present at the courthouse to research records to determine ownership of mineral rights. Old records may still either be in the physical book form or on microfiche or on a computer in some assessors' offices. It may be necessary to go to someone's home or ranch to get a lease signed. Much of the work can be accomplished on the phone or by computer and leases can be sent by mail.

Company landmen research ownership of mineral rights, find owners and heirs, negotiate with other companies and individuals, and write contracts to acquire mineral right leases.

Independent field landmen normally serve clients on a consulting contract basis. They research courthouse records to determine ownership of mineral rights and land. They locate mineral and surface owners and negotiate oil and gas leases. They obtain the necessary documents, prepare reports, and conduct surface inspections before drilling.

Equipment

The equipment is minimal: a computer, printer, fax, phone, and Internet connection. A laptop computer would be preferable over a desktop since some travel is required. You need to be able to type agreements, contracts for owners, cover letters, and print or email bills. You may want a program such as stamps.com to print postage and alleviate standing in line at the post office. Subscriptions to several databases may be required to search for owners or their heirs. Much of your research will be done online.

- Computer (laptop preferred)
- Printer
- Phone
- Fax
- Word Processing Software
- Internet Connection
- Ancestry and Graveyard Data Bases

Associations

American Association of Professional Landmen (AAPL) -- http://www.landman.org/wcm/aapl/

This website will give you a more in depth idea of what is involved in being a landman. Note that you do not need to be certified in order to be a landman. Sometime in the future there may be a requirement that you be certified or have a license but if you get in now, and are working in the field you should be grandfathered in later.

There are some home study landman courses. An inexpensive online course can be found on my website. This course gives a good background and idea of what you would be doing as a landman.

Income

A landman can make from $70,000 to over $130,000 per year with limited previous experience. There are no businesses I can think of where you can earn this kind of living without having worked in the field for a number of years and have a substantial amount of training.

Medical Transcription

Medical transcription is the process of converting physician or health care providers' dictations into text formats. Medical transcriptionists interpret and transcribe dictation, either from notes or from recordings. Transcriptionists must have expertise in medical language and health care documentation as well as grammar, spelling, formatting, and punctuation skills.   Notes may be about diagnosis, prognosis, courses of action, assessments, workups, or therapeutic procedures. These notes must be transcribed into a clearly written medical record.

Patient records are vital to health care providers. Patient's records must be kept for a variety of purposes. Providers use records for their reference, patient history, insurance purposes, and in the event of lawsuits.

It was thought with the emergence of voice recognition software that transcription would become obsolete but that did not happen. While voice recognition is helpful, many mistakes are made and the final product still has to be corrected. Without the original recording, it might be difficult to understand what was meant on the transcript made with voice recognition.

Skills

If you already have a background in medical terminology you are ready to start your own business. Most of the large agencies that hire at-home medical transcriptionists will not hire a person who has not had a course and/or real-time medical transcription experience at a hospital or doctor's office. Before attempting to start a home-based transcription business, it is best to work outside the home a couple of years to acquire experience.

Take a course. There are no official educational requirements to become a medical transcriptionist. There are many short programs that teach how to transcribe medical records, use specialized words and abbreviations, and use computer programs needed to upload the information. If you know the basics of medical terminology, some offices may be willing to train you in the profession, especially if they already have someone there who can act as a mentor.

Learn medical terminology. If you have no medical background, try catching up by buying books on the subject or taking a class that covers the basics. Many of these classes are available online.

Promote yourself by bringing your resume to local medical offices, hospitals and dentists. Offer your services as an add-on to whatever they already have, such as taking surplus work or last-minute transcriptions. Develop a website to advertise your services.

Equipment

You will need a quiet office space where you can focus on your work and hear the voice recordings clearly. A good set of medical reference books is also helpful.

- Desktop or Laptop Computer
- Headphones
- Printer
- Fax
- Phone
- Software
- Word Processing Software
- Medical Terminology Software
- Equipment to replay dictations

Income

Transcriptionists salaries range from $2,000 to $4,500 per month. The industry standard is to charge by the line of type produced. Some prices are calculated by the page, character, hour, or audio minute. Offshore transcriptionists charge considerably less but mistakes and dealing with someone whose first language is not English could be costly for a doctor if mistakes are made.

Organizations

Association for Healthcare Documentation Integrity (AHDI) http://www.ahdionline.org/

The AHDI was formerly the American Association for Medical Transcription. AHDI advocates workforce development and credentialing in allied health and the critical role of the technology-enabled documentation.

Mortgage Brokers

A mortgage broker is the middleman between borrowers and lenders. They are independent contractors who research available loans from a variety of lenders, possibly as many as 40 wholesale lenders at a time. Brokers seek a mortgage that satisfies the needs of a particular client. A mortgage broker is paid a fee (commission) which is typically based on the amount borrowed.

Mortgage brokers are involved in a lot of decision making. You will be an integral part in the tradition of homeownership by helping individuals decide which loan to use when purchasing homes. If you work on the commercial side of real estate, you will aid businesses in obtaining their loans. Many brokers start out working for a firm to gain experience and build a client base, and later work independently.

Skills

The requirements and training needed to become a mortgage broker varies from state to state. It is best to check with the government agency in your state responsible for licensing mortgage brokers to ensure that you fully understand the specific requirements in your area. While one state may ask nothing more than a fee to obtain a license, another state may require extensive classroom education, specific education experience, and even a minimum net worth. A few states also require background checks to ensure a potential mortgage broker has not been charged with crimes including fraud.

Most commonly, a person will be required to fill out an application, pay an application fee, meet minimum financial requirements and post a surety bond. A surety bond, which may also be known more specifically as a mortgage broker bond, covers clients (not the broker) in the event of a claim. Bonds are available from a number of major insurance companies and can be issued in a wide variety of dollar amounts, typically from $5,000 to more than $50,000, depending on the state the broker is doing business in.

 Contact the licensing entity in your state for detailed information for specific professional background requirements. The most common professional experiences accepted for mortgage brokers includes previous work in the money lending industry such as a loan officer, mortgage banker, or lender bank manager. Other acceptable backgrounds may include being a mortgage broker in another state or an attorney certified by any state as a real estate specialist.

Education requirements also vary by state and can include classroom instruction or practical hands-on experience as well as a passing grade on a school or state exam. For states that require classroom instruction, this requirement may often be met by attending classes at a local college, university, business or real estate school.

When hiring mortgage brokers, mortgage brokerage firms and mortgage lenders typically look for individuals with previous sales experience, a college degree or equivalent, computer and typing skills, and the ability to work flexible hours, including some nights and weekends.

Whether working for a firm or for yourself, you will eventually have to become licensed to be a mortgage broker. To find the licensing requirements for your location, look at a national trade association such as the National Association of Mortgage Brokers (NAMB) in the U.S. or the Canadian Institute of Mortgage Brokers and Lenders. The Web sites of these agencies can provide you with a list of licensing information broken down by state or province

Some states work with the National Mortgage Licensing System (NMLS) to provide their licenses. The NMLS allows an individual to become licensed in multiple states with one application. Most states either participate in the NMLS or are going to participate at some point.

Equipment

Office space is needed where you can meet with clients. If you meet with clients on a regular basis, there might be a zoning problem with people coming and going. It may be necessary to rent a small office or have an office with a separate entrance to your home with proper zoning.

- Desktop or Laptop Computer
- Printer
- Fax
- Phone
- Software

- Word Processing Software

Associations

National Association of Mortgage Brokers (NAMB) --
http://www.namb.org/namb/Default.asp

Agencies such as the National Association of Mortgage Brokers (NAMB) offer credentials that help brokers let potential consumers know that they have a certain minimum level of expertise. Even if it is not required in your state, certification can assist you in getting a job with a broker group or make you stand out to a consumer. There are three credentials available depending on your experience:

- GMA--General Mortgage Associate credential (beginning broker)
- CRMS--Certified Residential Mortgage Specialist (for those with 2 years of experience)
- CMC--Certified Mortgage Consultant (for professionals with 5 years-plus experience)

NAMB also offers continuing education courses to help navigate the newest lending options.

Income

Certified brokers earn an average salary of between $124,000 and $161,000. The mean average salary for non-certified brokers is around $100,000.

A number of mortgage brokers are also licensed as real estate brokers, offering mortgage services as supplements to realty services. Some states prohibit the addition of mortgage broker services to a real estate practice. Verify restrictions with your state's licensing agency.

Research & Data Services

If you love research, you may want to turn your abilities into a Research & Data Services business, also called an information broker. Your business can serve other businesses or individuals who need assistance in locating specific information. The key is to find your niche. With the advent of the Internet, it might be thought that research services are obsolete but that is far from the truth. Researching specialized information requires time and knowledge of how to conduct research, which a business or individual may not have. Choose your niche from the knowledge you already have or you can take classes, buy an online course, or purchase a book to learn how this business works. Choosing the right niche will result in a lucrative business.

Skills

Specialty skills will be needed for the niche you choose. Maybe you have previously worked for a title company or a law firm. You will need to be able to find, organize, analyze and package the information in a useful way for your client.

Some databases charge by the hour and are expensive which requires you to be proficient in their use. The less you pay for databases, the more profit your business will make. The majority of databases are online and their use will be the largest expense for this business. Examples of databases are Lexis-Nexis and WestLaw, which contain abstracts or the full text of articles from thousands of publications around the world, including major newspapers, magazines, newsletters, public records, court dockets, congressional bills, and much more.

Specialize in a certain type of information. Your niche may be abstracting, legal research, market research, real estate research, statistics, or scientific data. Listed below is a short list of some of the services you can offer.

- Research abstracts for real estate or mineral right titles
- Background research about a new product concept
- Patent search on a product your client wants to produce
- Research competitors producing related products for design and price information
- Research your client's competitors
- Real estate title parcel, as well as information about original cost, annual tax liability and other pertinent information
- Financial data and survey results for public relations and advertising
- Legal research relating to similar cases
- Research for hospitals and medical associations in medical research, such as data on new drugs or the latest techniques for certain procedures
- Assisting students and academics collecting information for writing or research projects
- Tracing family histories through extensive records that are available on databases
- Research for title insurance companies

While you will normally work regular business hours, be prepared to work evenings and weekends if you are facing a deadline to submit your research.

Equipment

Quiet office space is needed where you can focus on your work since researching is a tedious job requiring concentration. You would only need specialty software if it was required for your research output. Specialty databases will be your largest expense.

- Desktop or laptop computer
- Printer

- Fax
- Phone
- Word processing software
- Specialty software
- Specialty databases
- Internet service

A website is also helpful for listing your qualifications and performance. Always carry business cards and brochures. Identify your type of client and network to establish personal contacts. Direct mail can be used in some cases. Join trade associations and professional organizations. Much of this business comes from word of mouth.

Income

This business should be able to generate profits of $35,000 to $70,000 the first year of operation. You can charge by the hour or job. The going rate is between $25 to $100 per hour, depending on your specialty. If pricing by the job, you will need experience to estimate how many hours the job will take, if specialized data bases are needed, and allowance for difficulties in searching for information. Costs for photocopying, printing, and postage are billed separately at cost or marked up 15 to 20 percent. Marked up costs should be included in the agreement. You should be compensated for copies, going to the post office and packaging reports.

After your startup year, and word has spread, your business can be lucrative earning $80,000 to $100,000 a year. Your specialty niche will have a direct affect on your income opportunities.

Associations

Association of Independent Information Professionals
http://www.aiip.org

Society of Competitive Intelligence Professionals
http://www.scip.org

Resume Writer

Resume Writing is a timely business for today's economy. Many people are searching for a job and need a new or first resume. A well-written resume will help a jobseeker receive a job offer they might not otherwise get. A resume provides the first impression for a hiring company. A well written resume is a potential door opener for a candidate.

Write a resume to highlight your client's achievements, academic and professional education, previous job experience, and skills in a manner that is suitable for the position they are seeking. A person may want to have several different resumes each slanted towards a slightly different job position. Highlight different skills needed for specific jobs. Your client may have many skills but the resume should focus on the qualifications relevant to the job the client is seeking.

While everyone can jot down details of their academics and professional milestones, creating a resume and cover letter that leaves a lasting impression is a special skill everyone does not possess. A resume writing service should create a resume that provides accurate details in a style that is easy to read and understand. Generally, a jobseeker needs a professional resume writer to increase the chances of getting an interview.

Read books on the art of writing resumes and keep updated with the new trends in resume styles. Methods and keywords are used by hiring people to sort resumes for interviews. A single missed keyword can cost an interview for your client.

Equipment

- Computer
- Printer
- Fax
- Telephone
- Word Processing Software
- Resume Software/Templates
- Internet Connectivity

The main cost to start a resume writing business is a computer and good quality printer. You will also need word processing software, resume writing software, templates and a fax. The fax would allow someone without a computer or Internet access to get information to or from you. You will need Internet connectivity and the ability to copy files to a CD.

Use either resume writing software with templates or make your own using Microsoft Word or WordPerfect. It is too time consuming to start formatting and writing each resume from scratch. More than one template is needed since the resume for an engineer is different than one for a manufacturing worker. You should have a selection of templates and know which one fits specific jobs.

Supplies include good quality paper, CD's and envelopes. When your business increases, it is a good idea to have a backup computer and printer in case you have an equipment failure while trying to meet a deadline. Backup your data often on a portable hard drive. You may also want to backup older data and store it on CD's or DVD's. Your client may come back to get another resume several years later or request a change on one you previously wrote. Having a copy means you don't have to start at square one for changes.

An account with a mailing service like stamps.com is a real time saver. You can package the resumes, cover letter and CD, if required, in an envelope.   Weigh the envelope and print your own postage. In most cases your mailman will pick them up and that will save a trip to the post office. Even if you have to go to the post office, you won't have to wait in line and can get a discount on some services by having your own account. You can usually save money on the cost of shipping envelopes by using free priority mail envelopes. These priority envelopes are stiffer and will protect the resumes you send from being crumpled. At present, the mailman is required to stop at your house or a location you specify within their distance rules to pick up priority mail packages. If you are gone or busy, you can have a weather proof box on your porch for the mail pick up. The postal pickup service is activated when you request pickup at your address online.

Your job is to sell the jobseeker's profile to the hiring company and help your client get an interview.   In order to save time, have your client complete a form that describes all of their qualifications, past jobs, skills, education, honors, and any other pertinent information. Compile all of the information in a format that is suitable for the position. The completed resume and cover letter (if required) is emailed to your client or printed copies can be mailed or picked up. Your client may also want a digital copy on a CD.

You may want to specialize in writing resumes for a particular industry especially if you are familiar with engineering, software, or federal jobs. These resumes sometime command a higher fee. It is important to be familiar with the industry and know the associated buzz words.

It is your responsibility to present the information correctly and not understate or overstate the facts. Learn the language of each type of position that you are writing resumes for so nothing is misrepresented. Clients' information should always be kept confidential. Do not share the names of clients with anyone. If you show a sample resume to anyone, remove the name, contact details, and any other personally identifiable details.

Performance is measured by the number of interviews your client is able to secure with the help of the resume. Try to get feedback from your clients to keep track of the success rate for the resumes you have written. Keep a portfolio of well-written resumes to show potential customers. Be sure to use fictional names, addresses and phone numbers to keep your client's information confidential.

Market your services by inserting a small ad in your local paper. Advertise your business to graduating college and vocational school classes. Employment agencies may allow you to offer your services to complement theirs. A website is also helpful for listing your qualifications and performance without divulging any client information. Testimonials from your successful clients can be used on your website. Always carry business cards. Remember, writing is your business, so have a professional business card.   You can also list your services for free on Craig's List online. Be careful of scams that arise from Craig's List and online sources. Word of mouth from satisfied customers can be your best advertisement. Ask your customers for referrals.

Income

Resume writing is usually priced as a package with a fixed price contingent on complexity. The cost of multiple printed copies should be included in the fixed price. Have separate price lists for customers who want additional copies or a digital copy. You could charge an hourly rate but most people want to know the total cost and cost of extras. Recent prices vary from a low of $100 to $800. The average is $250 for 20 copies and 2 cover letters. Higher salary technical resumes are averaging $650. If you have good writing skills, a resume writing business can make an excellent living.

Associations

Resume writing is a home based business that can be started without formal qualifications. There are several organizations such as the National Resume Writers' Association and Professional Association of Resume Writers and Career Coaches who provide certifications such as Nationally Certified Resume Writer, Certified Professional Resume Writer etc. Getting a certification from any of these organizations and becoming a certified professional resume writer will add credibility to your business but is not really needed.

National Resume Writer's Association -- www.thenrwa.com
Professional Association of Resume Writers -- www.parw.com

Social Media Marketing Assistant

Social media marketing is the rage today. Businesses are willing to pay very well for this service and many who have these skills take them for granted. They have no idea how much money they could be making by offering their social media skills to businesses.

The social media world is growing, and most business owners don't have time to keep up. You can create a business as a social media marketing assistant or strategist if you have strong writing skills and a working knowledge of the major social media networking sites. Copy editing skills also are in demand for customers with blogs. Prior experience in public relations and marketing can also set you apart from those who just know social media tools. This business involves helping clients develop a social media strategy, build blogs, and set up Facebook Fan Pages, Twitter accounts, Linkedin profiles and Google+ accounts. If you know how to set up and maintain WordPress websites (they are free), you can specialize in that service and charge an even higher hourly rate. You can show small-business clients how to make social media marketing less intimidating. Pick up a niche for the type of customers you want. Be willing to do the first few jobs for free to get references. The key to being successful as a social media marketing consultant is keeping your skills updated and making sure you stay on top of the constantly changing features on the social networking sites.

Skills

You probably know much more about social media than you think. If you use Facebook, Linkedin, or Twitter, you already have many of the skills to be a Social Media Marketing Consultant. You will need to learn how to get results for the businesses you represent, not just chat with friends. It is also a plus to have experience in WordPress. You can easily build a blog or website for your client and the online version is free.

You can charge as much or as little as you want as a social media consultant. If you do the first few jobs for free, you will have references and feel more qualified and confident to go after larger clients. Do some research in your area to see what the going rate is. You may be surprised to see the minimum is $125 per hour. The industry average is $100 to $300 per hour. Once you get some experience you can raise your rate and lower your client load.

When you become overwhelmed with work, you can find qualified people to do the actual work on sites like Elance and Guru mentioned in Chapter 9, Freelance Marketplace, of this book. This will allow you time to seek more customers.

Social Media Consulting is still a wide open field. There are a number of books and courses that will get you up to speed quickly. You can first train yourself by setting up an account with each of the social media sites (Facebook, Linkdin, Twitter.) Set up your account with WordPress and build your own site. You will also need a YouTube account and a PayPal account.

WordPress has a great tutorial and you can learn how to use it for blogs only or to easily build a complete website quickly. Set all these sites up for yourself, just as you would for a customer. Study other people's blogs to see what kind of information is out there.

Equipment

- Computer
- Printer
- Fax
- Telephone
- Word Processing Software
- Internet Connectivity

You will need to have your own domain name and website. Think about whether you want to be a personal name brand or business brand. This would be either "Your Name" or your business name such as " PDS Consulting" or "Pat's Social Media" or "Pat Online." See what domains are available for the name you want. Purchase that domain name and then set up a WordPress account. Go through the online training and you will have your own website and blog before you know it.

Next set up your accounts on Facebook, Twitter, Linkdin, and YouTube. If you don't already know how to use them, most have good training articles or videos.

Last, set up a PayPal account in the name you have picked for your business. You may want to use PayPal to be paid for some of your work or to pay any freelancers that you may hire. Setting everything up in advance allows you to be ready to use any of the accounts or be paid without stumbling and having to tell a customer that you don't have an account yet. If you already have a PayPal account in your personal name, you are allowed to have one more for your business. Be aware that you will have to use a different bank account at a different bank from your personal account.

Create a solid positive presence for yourself online. Get traffic to your website and get customers. In order to try this opportunity before you leap into it yourself, look at the freelance section of this book. There will be job opportunities for social media listed on the different sites and you can check them out. You may even want to try doing one of them before venturing out on your own. There are a number of good books and courses you can take on social media.

Income

The average salary for a job in social media is $55,000 a year. Consultants earn much more commanding $100 to $300 per hour and some even earn more.

Website Design & Management

Starting a web design business may be easy for those who are already familiar with the website building or have a degree in a related subject. Designing and managing websites can be a very lucrative business. A large percentage of all businesses have websites. New businesses often do not have the time or expertise to build or manage their own site.

Both the freelance and the corporate world of web design usually mean long hours. Freelancers often work longer hours and are on call 24 hours a day. If you have designed a storefront for your client it is imperative for the site to stay up and functioning. Your client will be losing money in sales when it is down.

Skills

You will be expected to produce the design and layout, manage information changes, perform the maintenance and navigability of the site. Consider expanding to offer additional services such as search engine submission and optimization. Most clients do not have the knowledge or the time to manage their website themselves and will be happy to pay extra for the service.

You should be able to do the full project from logo design, web design, cutup (slicing), CMS (content management system) Integration and finally building out the content and launching it.

You may need to have a graphic designer make the logo or farm it out. If you do not understand what some of the jargon is, this business would not be for you. You can take classes online or at your local college but your client will expect you to be able to build his website without paying to train you.

Equipment

A web design business does not need a lot of equipment. One of the most important aspects of the business is having a good backup system. Having to rebuild a client's website is time consuming. Your choice of website building software will be important.

- Computer
- Backup Hard Drive
- Printer
- Fax
- Telephone
- Word Processing Software
- Website Building Software
- Internet Connectivity

In the past, web designers created websites completely from scratch. Now, it makes more sense to buy a template and then adapt it to the needs of the client. This is a great time saver and an option to consider.

The first step is to set up your own business website. Make sure your website looks professional and has no mistakes. Build a portfolio and with permission, list the websites you have designed on your website. This way your prospective clients can see your work. While you can start by designing the website of a friend or family member, consider offering your services to a nonprofit organization, such as a church, senior organization, or local clinic. Not only will you be doing a good deed, but the reference will look impressive in your resume.

If you have a day job and want extra income and a chance to test the waters as a web designer, consider freelancing part time. This way, you can see if you will have enough work building up to switch to full time and also if it is a business that you enjoy.

Income

Web Designers make an income between $35,000 to $98,000. The average hourly income for freelance web designers is between $30 and $100 per hour. A freelance web designer has the ability to make a higher income by setting their own fees and having a low overhead.

The high and low salary has a large range which is tied to the difficulty of the different types of web design. The title 'web designer' covers descriptions from simple page layout to advanced graphic design and CSS (Cascading Style Sheets) to complicated server-side language knowledge that includes Perl, Cold Fusion, PHP/MySQL, or ASP. Your income will depend on where you live and whether you are seeking employment or are a freelance web designer.

Word of mouth is the largest contributor to freelancers getting work. Friends, other professionals, and work you have done in the past will draw the most new clients. A large amount of work can also be picked up from social media and networking. Job boards with work for web designers are listed below.

FreelanceSwitch – http://jobs.freelanceswitch.com/
AuthenticJobs – http://www.authenticjobs.com/
Krop – http://www.krop.com/
Smashing Jobs – http://jobs.smashingmagazine.com/
Designm.ag Job board – http://designm.ag/jobs/
Design jobs on the wall – http://jobs.webdesignerwall.com/

Associations

American Association of Web Designers --
http://aawebmasters.com/
American Association of Web Masters --
http://aawebmasters.com/
 American Institute of Graphic Arts -- http://www.aiga.org/

NOTE: Please refer to my websites for business resources, books, courses, software, equipment and supplies for the businesses in this book.   From time to time additional business opportunities will be posted on my website. I hope this information makes the research for your new business easier. Clicking on the links in the websites will take you to resources for each item.

> http://www.pdsloss.com/
> http://www.RealisticHomeBusinesses.com/

Chapter 9

Freelance Marketplace

Many professionals work on a project by project basis as an independent contractor. Some businesses prefer to hire independent contractors on an as-needed basis. By hiring a consultant by the project, an employer does not have the responsibilities or expenses required with full-time employees. Benefits such as health insurance, disability insurance, eye and dental insurance, vacation, and workman's comp insurance are expensive. Hiring an independent contractor is desirable for short term jobs especially when it is uncertain how long the job will last. Keep in mind that doing an exceptional job is likely to pave the pathway for your services in the future and may result in full-time employment at a later date.

You can look at the freelance projects available in your field and bid on the projects that apply to your services or abilities. You will be in competition with other freelancers from all over the world. Fees may not be equal to what freelancers might earn from a private non-bid project. The person hiring will list their jobs from small to large. Bids are reviewed and the recipient is chosen. Selection is not always made on price. Qualifications, background, language, and skills are also taken into consideration. Positive feedback on previous jobs will also help tip the scale in your favor.

When you bid on a job, calculate all of your expenses, which includes an acceptable wage along with extras such as insurance, and reflect your value on the project. Your fee should be competitive with other bidders who have similar qualifications that are bidding on the project. Pay close attention to the time frame required to complete the project, which you will be expected to meet.

Open a PayPal account. PayPal is a payment processor commonly used for online business. PayPal is a secure way to send money and more importantly get paid quickly. Many online businesses pay people for services via PayPal and you can deposit your money into your bank account within days.

Each freelance marketplace will have a section where you will fill out a profile. Take your time writing your profile. Your profile is your online "resume" that all prospective employers will be reviewing along with fellow freelancers. Fellow freelancers can also be a significant source of referrals and direct work. Spend a lot of time polishing your summary describing your accomplishments, qualifications, background, language, and skills.

The person hiring you will rank your performance on the job you do for them. Provide a job well done, excellent communication, service and deliver your project on time. Your feedback performance for completed work will be displayed on your profile for all future employers to see. It is best to go the extra mile on your commitments which should keep your rating high.

I suggest getting an EIN (Employer Identification Number) instead of using your social security number. This is not only more professional but protects your social security number. See Chapter 15, How to Structure Your Business, for instructions on how to get an EIN from the IRS. It is simple and quick to do. You are normally paid by the freelance company and at the end of the year you will receive a 1099 for tax purposes.

The freelance sites make money by charging a fee on each job. Memberships are sometimes free but the percent assessed for the job fee is larger. You can pay a membership fee in order to bring down the percent of the fee per job. All fees are different for each company and subject to change so make sure to review any new or changed fees. Most freelance sites offer an escrow service to hold payments and protect both parties.

New contractors often price themselves a little below the average market rate to enhance their chances of landing their first jobs. Once they have established a work history with positive feedback, they have proven themselves and can justify bidding higher rates.

Monitoring software is now used on a number of freelance sites and might be considered intrusive in tracking the work habits of freelancers.

The following freelance sites described are some of the most well known but there are more in the market place. These sites provide a thriving international marketplace for numerous different types of projects.

Elance.com

Elance states: "While global economies continue to struggle with job creation, online work thrived this year with 650,000 new jobs posted, and cumulative earnings set to surpass $500 million. The number of businesses hiring on Elance and the number of online professionals working on Elance grew more than 120%." Their site claims 130,000 active clients and 550,000 active contractors.

- Programmers
- Designers
- Writers
- Marketers

- Admins
- Consultants
- Finance

After you create your profile, clients looking for your skills will be able to find and hire you. Alternatively, you can simply check out one of the jobs posted every day and submit up to 10 proposals each month. There are also membership plans if you would like to connect with more prospective clients.

Fees

When you quote an hourly rate or a fixed price to a client, Elance automatically includes a service fee of 8.75%. After Elance bills clients and receives payment for the work you perform, the fee is deducted and the rest is immediately transferred to you. In other words, the cost of using Elance is included in the price you quote and Elance only makes money when you get paid for the work.

You may work by the hour or project. Elance has time sheet tools to track your hourly time worked. This monitoring software is now used on a number of freelance sites and might be considered intrusive in tracking the work habits of freelancers. Elance offers a licensed Escrow service to protect you when working online.

Guru.com

Statistics show 1 million users worldwide have used guru.com to complete over 3 million tasks, share over seven million messages and files, and create over 150 million dollars in value.

You create your profile, submit proposals, and are selected by an employer. The next step is to request a deposit, complete the work and receive payment. Once a project is awarded to you, you use Guru's SafePay service requesting a deposit for 100% of the project's value before proceeding with the work. The funds are held in a secure account pending work completion. As completed work is approved by your employers, funds will be released to your cash account.   Withdraw payments by a method of your choice: direct deposit, PayPal, prepaid MasterCard, check and wire transfer are available.

Listed below are the popular job listings on Guru.com. The numbers of available jobs derived from their website was current at the time this book was written. There are also more categories and subcategories than the ones listed below.

Popular Jobs on Guru

- Websites & Ecommerce (1,449)
- Programming & Databases (964)
- Engineering & CAD (83)
- Networking & Telephone Systems (69)
- ERP & CRM (33)
- Graphic Design & Multimedia (436)
- Writing, Editing & Translation (731)
- Illustration & Art (178)
- Photography & Videography (57)
- Fashion & Interior Designs (34)
- Broadcasting (27)
- Admin Support (140)
- Marketing & Communications (126)
- Sales & Telemarketing (219)
- Business Consulting (65)
- Legal (52)
- Finance & Accounting (39

Fees

Listed information was taken from Guru's website. Please check their website for changes in fees or payment methods.

The cost of our service depends on your membership level.

- Membership Type — select a membership level for every profile you post.
  - Basic membership is free.
  - Guru membership fees range from $9.95 to $34.95 per month.
  - Guru Vendor membership fees range from $12.94 to $45.44 per month.
  - Annual memberships can be purchased at a 50% discount. An additional 20% discount is offered when upgrading more than one profile at a time.

- Project Fee — We charge all Freelancers either a 4.5% or 9% project fee based on profile membership type.
  - Guru and Guru Vendor members pay 4.5% project fee.
  - Basic members pay 9% project fee.

The fee is subtracted from the total amount the Employer's invoice payment or release from SafePay.

- Payment Processing Fee — We also charge all Freelancers a 2.95% payment processing fee to cover the costs of payment processing, credit card fees, and PayPal fees. The fee is subtracted from the total amount an Employer pays through Guru.com.
- Freelancer Payment Method Fees — You may be charged a small processing fee depending on the payment method you've selected for us to pay you.

Start with a free registration until you learn the ropes. After you are comfortable and have completed a few jobs, a paid membership may be worth the investment. This will reduce the commission rate and allows you some extra options.

o-Desk.com

o-desk describes itself as "an online staffing marketplace and management platform that provides a convenient way to hire, manage, and pay individuals no matter where they are located. Businesses are no longer limited to local talent or traditional hiring cycles. With a thriving online workforce available on-demand, you can post a job for free, field applications in hours and rapidly hire the best person for the job, regardless of where in the world they happen to be."

Search for jobs By Category or browse by Skill. The numbers in parenthesis were jobs available when researching o-Desk.

Categories

Web Development
Web Design (4864)
Web Programming (7668)
Ecommerce (1206)
UI Design (271)
Website QA (151)
Website Project Management (437)
Other - Web Development (1641)

Software Development
Desktop Applications (715)
Game Development (301)
Scripts & Utilities (471)
Software Plug-ins (227)
Mobile Apps (1924)
Application Interface Design (179)
Software Project Management (97)
Software QA (82)
VOIP (92)
Other - Software Development (958)

Networking & Information Systems
Network Administration (154)
DBA - Database Administration (104)
Server Administration (333)
ERP / CRM Implementation (54)
Other - Networking & Information Systems (251)

Writing & Translation
Technical Writing (554)
Website Content (1242)
Blog & Article Writing (3153)
Copywriting (401)
Translation (667)
Creative Writing (641)
Other - Writing & Translation (874)

Administrative Support
Data Entry (1324)
Personal Assistant (1056)
Web Research (771)
Email Response Handling (71)
Transcription (213)
Other - Administrative Support (696)

Design & Multimedia
Graphic Design (2386)
Logo Design (876)
Illustration (380)
Print Design (331)
3D Modeling & CAD (338)
Audio Production (113)
Video Production (673)
Voice Talent (175)
Animation (361)
Presentations (191)

Engineering & Technical Design (97)
Other - Design & Multimedia (500)

Customer Service
Customer Service & Support (295)
Technical Support (96)
Phone Support (125)
Order Processing (42)
Other - Customer Service (88)

Sales & Marketing
Advertising (514)
Email Marketing (339)
SEO - Search Engine Optimization (2503)
SEM - Search Engine Marketing (394)
SMM - Social Media Marketing (934)
PR - Public Relations (135)
Telemarketing & Telesales (703)
Business Plans & Marketing Strategy (184)
Market Research & Surveys (196)
Sales & Lead Generation (1057)
Other - Sales & Marketing (611)

Business Services
Accounting (185)
Bookkeeping (144)
HR / Payroll (27)
Financial Services & Planning (82)
Payment Processing (14)
Legal (158)
Project Management (112)
Business Consulting (130)
Recruiting (103)
Statistical Analysis (72)
Other - Business Services (567)

Fees

Neither the freelancer nor the employer pays anything to sign up with oDesk. There are no fees for posting jobs, creating profiles, applying for jobs, or conducting interviews. oDesk makes money only when the employer pays for work done by freelancers. Freelancers get 90% of the advertised rates and oDesk retains the remaining 10%. This is true for all payments, whether they are hourly rates, fixed price jobs or bonuses.

The oDesk Team application takes snapshots of your desktop six times an hour, and tells you when it is doing so. You can see those snapshots in your Work Diary and even delete the shot for a given block of time. Your activity level is logged in terms of frequency of keyboard and mouse clicks, but there is no keystroke logging or any other kind of data gathering. o-Desk has verified time sheet tools to track your hourly time worked. This monitoring software is now used on a number of freelance sites and might be considered intrusive in tracking the work habits of freelancers.

Payment

For U.S.-based freelancers, o-Desk can deposit your earnings directly into your bank account. For U.S. and international contractors, o-Desk offers Skrill (formerly Moneybookers), wire transfers and the Payoneer debit MasterCard, which works everywhere a regular MasterCard would work.

At the end of the year, o-Desk will furnish a 1099. Taxes are not withheld and you are responsible for making quarterly tax payment. o-Desk may have a health plan you can apply for.

This is the o-Desk printed guarantee from their website: "oDesk will guarantee payment to Contractors working on Hourly-Rate Contracts where the Employer has a verified payment method, the time represented is tracked using the oDesk Team software, the work performed and captured pertains directly to the Contract billed, and each Time Log is annotated with appropriate work memos describing the work performed. Determination of whether these criteria have been met is at the sole discretion of oDesk. The Payment Guarantee will not apply to Contractors or Contracts in violation of this Agreement, where the Contractor is aware of or complicit in another User's violation of this Agreement, or where there is any other involvement in fraudulent activities or abuse of this Payment Guarantee."

Since o-Desk does not require employers to deposit funds before the work is started, you will want to check their guarantee before you work for them. I have personally met people who have done a considerable amount of work through o-Desk and never had a problem but all online work should be thoroughly checked out prior to starting work.

LiveWork.com

LiveWorks comes from LiveOps, a Silicon Valley company, which is known for its virtual call center operations. LiveWorks describes itself as: "The LiveOps cloud contact center offering provides a total solution – spanning from technology to talent to provide your enterprise choice – choice in how you source and deliver services to your clients. Our LiveOps Platform, LiveOps Applications and LiveOps Talent meets the challenges facing your contact center today and will transform your customer interactions in the cloud."

The company has more than 20,000 home-based agents across the United States servicing more than 250 global companies. Their teams of independent contractors can take on projects of any size. They refer to Internet-oriented solutions as "cloudsourcing" which means instantly sending projects of any size to workers anywhere.

LiveOps matches the best available independent, at-home agents to each customer interaction using a pay-per-use model. Every interaction – regardless of type – is centrally routed, managed, tracked, and rendered reportable in real time.

At this time, LiveOps does not charge a fee to join or a contractor's fee but all independent contractors who provide services for clients must pass a background and credit check. This check is administered by FirstAdvantage, who requires $50 for both the background and credit checks. FirstAdvantage is a partner of LiveOps. LiveWork charges a service fee of 10% from the amount paid by the client.

There is a telephone requirement to use a corded phone (no cordless phones) using a separate landline from your personal phone. A desktop or laptop is also required with DSL or cable modem Internet connection. You must be connected to your computer by cable, no wireless. Look on their site for more specifics. You must be a legal resident of the U.S.

Independent Agents submit invoices for their services using an online system. LiveOps pays submitted invoices by either check or direct deposit, on the 1st and 16th of the month. The fees paid cover services provided in the two weeks prior to the payment date.

iFreelance.com

iFreelance describes itself as: "The premier place for independent professionals looking for freelance work. Whether you have experience in proofreading, art jobs or data entry, iFreelance is the hub where you can meet entrepreneurs and sell your freelancing skills."

Categories

- Accounting / Finance
- Administrative Support

- Business Consulting
- Engineering / Architecture
- Graphic Design / Multimedia
- Legal
- Marketing / Advertising / Sales
- Networking / Hardware / Telephony
- Photography / Videography
- Programming / Database Development
- Traditional Art (Illustration / Painting)
- Training / Education
- Writing / Editing / Translation

Popular Freelance Projects

Website Design (28)
Logo Design (21)
Website Programming (16)
Other Graphic Design (9)
Book Illustration (8)

Fees

Freelancers pay a monthly subscription to create profiles and bid on projects. iFreelance doesn't charge commissions or transaction fees. Both sides get a better deal. At the time it appears there is not an abundance of jobs listed on this site.

Freelancer.com

Freelancer.com (previously called GetAFreelancer) is a marketplace for buyers and sellers of IT services. Freelancer describes their services as: "We connect over 3,111,738 employers and freelancers globally from over 234 countries & regions. Through our website, employers can hire freelancers to do work in areas such as software, writing, data entry and design right through to engineering and the sciences, sales and marketing, and accounting

& legal services." This company is based in Australia. There is a global freelancer mix that you will be bidding against in many other parts of the world.

The statistics for this site are updated in real time. There were 3,111,755 users, $114,905,540 U.S.D. earned, and 1,401,661 projects when the research was done on this site. The numbers in parenthesis are the jobs available at the time this site was researched.

Categories

- Website IT & Software
- Mobile
- Writing
- Design
- Data Entry
- Product Sourcing & Manufacturing
- Sales & Marketing
- Business, Accounting & Legal

Top Categories Available

PHP (2340)
Internet Marketing (1317)
MySQL (781)
Facebook (495)
Software Architecture (405)
Leads (342)
eCommerce (306)
Photoshop (266)
Joomla (210)
Web Search (190)
HTML5 (157)

Telemarketing (129)
Animation (113)
Affiliate Marketing (107)
XXX (94)
Website Design (1772)
Excel (882)
Marketing (650)
Copywriting (491)
iPhone (389)
AJAX (334)
Android (296)
Bulk Marketing (258)
C# Programming (207)
Shopping Carts (180)
Twitter (154)
Translation (127)
Copy Typing (113)
Proofreading (106)
3D Animation (91)
Data Entry (1738)
SEO (871)
Link Building (603)
.NET (485)
Social Networking (382)
BPO (328)
Logo Design (295)
Article Submission (236)
C++ Programming (205)
Virtual Assistant (170)
jQuery / Prototype (143)
eBay (125)
Visual Basic (111)
SQL (102)
Script Install (91)
HTML (1619)
Articles (871)

Article Rewriting (528)
Advertising (477)
Sales (378)
Academic Writing (324)
CSS (278)
Flash (222)
iPad (197)
C Programming (168)
Research (139)
Web Scraping (116)
Anything Goes (110)
Objective C (97)
3D Modeling (89)
Graphic Design (1459)
Data Processing (792)
Javascript (498)
Mobile Phone (431)
Wordpress (346)
Blog (308)
Ghostwriting (276)
Java (213)
Reviews (191)
Technical Writing (162)
ASP (132)
Video Services (115)
Illustrator (108)
Linux (95)
3D Rendering (88)

Fees

Joining and bidding on projects are both free. Free members are charged $5.00 or 10%, whichever is higher, per project. A Gold Membership is US $24.95 per month and your project commissions drop to 3%. Note that Australian customers are required to pay an extra 10% GST on all fees.

Payment

Each registered Freelancer.com member is provided with a free online account for fund transfers. Funds can be added as direct payments from other members, or from various sources, including the member's credit card, online accounts such as PayPal, Skrill (formerly Moneybookers), or by bank wire transfer. A member may withdraw funds from his or her account via wire transfer or direct deposit to an online account (PayPal, Skrill (formerly Moneybookers). An optional debit card is also available that provides members with immediate access to the funds in their accounts.

Withdrawal transfers are handled on a weekly basis. Minimal fees to offset processing costs may apply to certain transfers and are deducted when the transfer is initiated. Fees payable to Freelancer.com for memberships, commissions, etc. are also deducted from members' accounts as applied.

Employers can pay service providers via transfer from their accounts to the accounts of the providers. Other methods of payment are also allowed at the mutual discretion of the service buyer and service provider. Though not required, payment via Freelancer.com offers advantages for both the employer and freelancer.

When a project is completed, if payment is made within the Freelancer.com system, the rating and feedback system for that project is activated. This provides the opportunity for the service buyer and service provider to rate each other's performance on a simple, 10-point scale as well as leave comments. To ensure fairness, members may also post a response to the other party's comments. A member's cumulative rating as well as individual project ratings and feedback are made available as part of the member's profile to help other members assess the value of working with that member.

The feedback and rating system allows both buyers and providers the opportunity to build their reputations through performance. It also provides the entire Freelancer.com community with added protection against potential scams and unsatisfactory business transactions.

vWorker.com

VWorker was previously RentACoder.com. The "v" in the new name stands for virtual. Offices are in Tampa, Florida. This site used to specialize in custom software projects but now has added more categories.

Listed below are the categories they had listed on their website. There were too many subcategories to list. The number in parenthesis after each category is a snapshot of the number of jobs available on the day the company research was done.

Categories

Administrative Support (130)
Business Services (176)
Design, art and audio-visual (441)
Technology (1300)
Writing and Translation (251)
Other (135)

vWorker allows you to require all workers who bid on your project to be Chaperon enabled. Chaperon makes it virtually impossible for a worker to copy or pirate your source code by protecting it from creation and transport to storage and retrieval.

vWorker's time card uses screenshots and a webcam to visually demonstrate what workers do. This monitoring software is now used on a number of freelance sites and might be considered intrusive in tracking the work habits of freelancers.

Fees

There are no charges to post a project, to select a worker, or to make a transaction. A fee of 15% is added to each project final bid to cover costs.

Payment

Payments to you are made through several methods, depending on where you live and which method you choose. Some of the methods are PayPal, Payoneer (prepaid debit/credit card or direct deposit), Skrill (formerly Moneybookers), snail mail, or Western Union. Most of these have a small processing fee. At year end, you will be sent a 1099-misc if you make over a dollar amount threshold set by the IRS.

vWorker escrows project funds to protect the parties and offers an arbitration process in the event of a dispute. Company statistics show 45% of workers arbitrations are completed under a day and 75% of them are completed under a week.

ScriptLance.com

This website specializes in programming, writing, design, and marketing projects. ScriptLance describes itself as: "R3N3 is an online business started by Canadian entrepreneur Rene Trescases in 1999. Incorporated in the province of Ontario, and operating out of Toronto, Canada, with offices in New Delhi and employees around the world. We have a long history of working with website programming technologies and freelance outsourcing. Started in 2001 as a way to satisfy the custom programming demands of our own clients, ScriptLance has become one of the Internet's most popular and successful software outsourcing marketplaces. Our service has helped thousands of entrepreneurs stay under budget and helped many freelance workers become more financially independent."

Categories

Programmers
- PHP
- MySQL
- Joomla
- Javascript
- XML
- Social Networking
- Modifications

Writers
- Blogs
- Article Writing
- Data Entry
- Article Submission
- Content Writing

All Job Types

Designers
- Website Design
- Logos
- Graphics
- HTML
- XHTML
- CSS
- Wordpress

Marketers
- Search Engine Optimization
- Links
- Link Building
- Twitter
- Facebook

Fees

There are no sign up fees and no monthly fees. Buyers can post projects and receive bids/quotes for free. Once the buyer selects a winning bid their account will be charged a flat fee of $5, which must be paid within 30 days. Fees are refunded if the project is cancelled. Programmers are charged a $5 or 5% fee (whichever is greater) when their bid is selected as the winner for a project. Programmers also have 30 days time to pay this fee, and it is refunded if the project is cancelled.

Payment

Methods of payment are: PayPal, Moneybookers, Payoneer debit card, Bank Wire, or Check (including FedEx delivery). ScriptLance offers a dispute resolution process.

crowdSPRING.com

This site specializes in logo and graphic design. The customer picks from 42 categories, names a price they are willing to pay, and sets a deadline. Sometimes as many as 110 freelancers submit their work. The customer chooses a designer to work with and perfect the design. The designer is not paid until the work is approved by the customer. There is a money back guarantee to the customer.

Instead of working with one or two designers and choosing from several designs, the customer will work with dozens of designers. The customer selects their favorite from an average of 110+ custom designs, and gets full rights to that design. This site appears to be similar to a contest between all of the designers or writers who apply.

Categories

Design
- Graphic Design
- Web Design
- Industrial
- Mobile

Writing Projects
- Naming
- Creative
- Business
- Online
- Editing & Proofreading

Fees

There is no fee for the freelancer to sign up and also no commission. There is a listing fee plus a 15% commission to host the project and give the customer access to over 108,318 designers and writers.

Payment

After the customer approves the final files during project wrap up, payment is processed within two business days if paying you by PayPal. Wire transfer payments are processed once per week.

NOTE: Please refer to my websites for business resources, books, courses, software, equipment and supplies for the businesses in this book.   From time to time additional business opportunities will be posted on my website. I hope this information makes the research for your new business easier. Clicking on the links in the websites will take you to resources for each item.

http://www.pdsloss.com/
http://www.RealisticHomeBusinesses.com/

Chapter 10

Mobile Professions

Handyman

A handyman business can be extremely profitable if you have the qualifications and experience. Many people are not capable of fixing problems around the home. Some people simply do not know how to do the job, some are not physically capable and others do not have the time or just do not want to do the job. They do not want to pay a contractor's rate to patch a hole in the wall or a plumber's rate to fix a leaky faucet. That leaves the handyman a perfect opportunity to pick up the jobs that have built up on someone's "to-do" list. You can bet if they like your work, you will be called back for more work. These customers will also recommend you to their friends.

Skills

A handyman business requires the experience to accomplish each job that is offered. You may need to fix a leaky faucet, replace an electrical plug, or replace a broken deck board. In some areas of the country, a contractor's license and a business license are required. Some jobs do not require a contractor's license. You can limit the work offered to jobs that can be done without a license. Check your local laws for the type of license needed.

Advertise in your local paper, through building supply stores, Craig's List, free papers, bank bulletin boards in laundromats, clubhouses, and anywhere with a bulletin board. Print business cards and give several to each customer for them to give to friends. If you want to specialize in only certain repairs, note your specialties on your business card and in ads. You may also want to create a brochure with your specialties listed. A good personality and being a people person is a plus for this job. Create a list of things you will and will not do. Let customers know if you will only do carpentry and plumbing but not electrical jobs. Make ads, flyers, and business cards clear to eliminate needless phone calls.

Here are some suggestions of services to offer:

- Repairs and Replacements
- Painting
- Power Washing
- Deck Staining
- Gutter Cleaning
- Install Closet Organizers
- Rental Property Repairs
- Attic Insulation
- Fall Cleanup
- Kitchen & Bath Updates
- Drywall

Equipment

A truck or van is needed to carry some of the materials to the customer's site along with tools. The correct tools for the job will make your job go smoother. Invest in good tools that will last and help perform the job easier and faster.

- Truck/Van
- Trailer
- Hand Tools

- Saws/Drills
- Compressor

Have proper business insurance and a business name to present yourself as a business. Check locally to see if a contractor's license and safety certificate are needed.

Income

Customers are happy to pay a handyman from $25 to $100 for a job that a contractor would charge much more to do. Rates depend on your location and sometimes the area of town where services are offered. Many customers will want to know what your flat fee is to complete a job. Work prices out ahead of time. Each job will be different but you should be able to tell about how many hours each job will take before starting. You can also give a customer a "not to exceed" estimate.

Find out what others in your area charge. Start your business by charging on the low end of the range and increase prices when business builds and you start receiving word of mouth referrals.

Home Inspector

Most homebuyers hire home inspectors to check the foundation, basement, attic, plumbing, electrical, roof, and other areas of the home to make sure it is not in need of major repairs. The home inspector creates a report based on their inspection of the home. Usually the sale of the home is contingent on the inspection results. The home inspector's report may prompt the buyers to ask the sellers to either make repairs or adjust the asking price if any major repairs are needed.

Many home inspectors also inspect apartment buildings and commercial property that are being sold. Inspecting multiple units will help your bottom line since you are only driving to one location.

Skills

Expertise in home construction and remodeling is needed for this business. Some states require a license. The association listed below offers training and testing to become certified. Apply for a business license. You may want to become a LLC, which is a Limited Liability Corporation to shield you from lawsuits. At a minimum, carry good errors and omissions insurance to help cover the costs of a lawsuit or settlement. Something could be missed in the inspection or it could be hidden. Insurance will limit financial exposure.

Equipment

A vehicle capable of carrying a ladder and tools is required. If you want to give your customer an instant report, a laptop and portable printer will be needed. Organize reports into binders with dividers for a professional looking report. A notebook or tape recorder is needed to record your inspection findings while walking around the house. Do not try to keep all of the details in memory.

- Vehicle capable of carrying a ladder
- Ladder
- Electrical meter
- Electrical tester
- Water test bottles
- Ozone test
- Tape measure
- Safety glasses
- Notebook or tape recorder
- Computer
- Fax
- Printer
- Binders
- Dividers
- Invoices

Market your services to real estate agents, real estate attorneys, and mortgage lenders. Place ads in your local paper, yellow pages, community bulletin boards and local business directories. Network with real estate agents and builders. Being listed as a member of the American Society of Home Inspectors (ASHI) listed below will be influential.

Income

The average home inspector's income is $62,000 a year. This figure can vary greatly depending on your location. A larger city with a greater number of homes, apartments, and commercial building sales will provide more opportunities.

Associations

American Society of Home Inspectors (ASHI) -- http://ashi.org/

Home Painting

Home painting is a popular business. Many people want their homes painted but either cannot physically do the job, do not have time, or do not want to take the time out of their life. You can specialize in outside home painting, inside painting, or a combination of both.

Skills

Painting requires physical strength and no fear of heights. Ask for references from satisfied customers since potential customers may ask for references. Learn how to mask windows and trim. There are tricks to the trade that make painting easier and faster. Check to see if your painting business will require special licenses.

Equipment

You will need a truck or van to haul ladders, tools and paint. You may want to keep your business books on a computer. Purchase liability insurance for your company and any hired workers. It is good to have insurance protection in case an accident occurs on the job site or causes damage to people or property. Customers may ask if you have liability insurance before they hire you.

- Truck or Van
- Scaffolds
- Ladders
- Plastic or fabric drop cloths
- Buckets
- Extension poles
- Painter's tape
- Pressure painter
- Brushes
- Coveralls

Income

The salary range is $20,000 to $62,000 a year for a painter. Your income will vary by location.   Doing a professional job and word of mouth is one of your best advertisements. Market your business by listing ads in your local newspaper, Craig's List, and local flyers or magazines. Print cards and flyers listing specialties. State references are available and that you have liability coverage. Homebuilders and real estate professionals are another source of new customers.

In-Home Caregivers

As the number of senior citizens increases, so does the demand for caregivers. Caregiving in the home can help ease the burden placed on family members to take care of the aged or disabled person in their family. When the person needing care is a family member, the task can become exhausting to the family who is managing the care for that person in either their own home or the family member's home. Having part-time or full-time help can alleviate the potential for going to a nursing home.

Individuals who provide in-home care are usually treated as independent contractors. This will help the aged or disabled avoid the additional burden of employment tax reporting. Certain qualifications must be met in order to be classified as an independent contractor. The caregiver generally serves more than one client, provides their own transportation between clients, and maintains their own liability insurance and business licenses. The caregiver requires no training or supervision, sets their own fees and availability, and is free to accept or decline a client.

Skills

This business requires a medical background. Certification is needed in most states to give medications. Knowing what to do in an emergency is imperative. Your background will dictate the type of care you can give from basic caregiver to registered nurse. Being a people person and compassionate is a must in this field. Your business will depend on how much your clients like the care you give.

If you are providing skilled medical care to clients, you will need to obtain the appropriate licenses to include Medicare and Medicaid certification. Requirements for a nonmedical business are not as strict. Check with your state to determine what licenses are required for your business.

Equipment

Dependable transportation to get to your client's home is required. Appointments are made by phone and should be kept in an appointment book.

- Vehicle
- Phone
- Appointment Book

Income

Income for this business ranges from $16,000 to $42,000. As with most businesses, your location will dictate your income. When you become well known and have a good reputation, your income will increase.

The current wage and hour law exempts domestic service employees who provide companionship services in a family home from minimum wage and overtime requirements. The worker's compensation law also provides an exemption for individuals employed in domestic service in or about the private home who are under private contract between the homeowner or agent of the homeowner, and the individual performing the work. Be sure to check the current law when you set up your business.

Landscaping/Lawn Services

As the baby boomer generation increases in number, the need for landscaping and lawn services will increase. Older people cannot always operate lawn mowers like they used to when they were younger. They will need assistance maintaining their lawns. Many younger people are busy working and do not have the time.

Skills

Physical ability is one of the most important skills in this business. By the end of the season, you should be in excellent shape from the manual labor required of landscaping. Decide what type of services to provide. Here are some ideas:

- Lawn mowing
- Garden tilling
- Sod installation/seeding
- Tree pruning

- Weeding, fertilizing, pest control
- Retaining walls
- Flower beds
- Rock with landscape fabric underneath
- Planting trees and plants
- Landscape maintenance
- Landscape design

This job requires professional mowing, trimming, pruning, and other services. Your skill level should be higher than an average person. Learn how to handle machinery and hazardous chemicals, and about horticulture. A special license is required if you are applying chemicals such as pesticides. Customers expect you to know what grows well in their soil, looks good, and is easy to care for. Landscaping can be expensive and people want to know they have hired a knowledgeable person.

Equipment

You may already have many of the tools you need in your garage. Almost everyone has rakes, shovels, clippers, loppers, and hand clippers. Most people have a lawn mower and possibly a riding lawn mower and tiller. Other items needed are a blower, broom wheelbarrow, tarps, and trash bags. When you first go into business, you can use many of the items you already have and add professional grade tools and mowers as business grows. Other equipment can be rented.

- Truck, SUV, or Van
- Trailer
- Lawn Mower
- Trimmers
- Tiller
- Skid loader (only for heavy work)
- Hand tools (shovels, rakes, etc.)
- Calendar or Schedule Book

Income

Most lawn service businesses make between $15 and $25 an hour. There is a wide range of income in the landscaping business from $5,000 to $160,000 a year. In colder climates, the earning season is shorter than in a warmer climate. Most jobs are billed by the job instead of by the hour. If your job requires materials, ask your customer to pay one half down upfront and the remainder paid upon completion. All of this should be in the initial contract with the customer which will protect both parties should there be any disagreement.   Businesses that include landscape design or chemical application earn more than businesses that only specialize in lawn services.

Hand business cards out to your family, friends and neighbors. Word of mouth will generate work and be your best advertisement. Give cards to local real estate offices, gardening centers, banks, and builders. Advertise in local papers and on Craig's List.   Other contacts include golf courses, rental properties, universities, cemeteries, historic buildings and other public places.

Maintenance/Janitorial/Custodial

If you do not mind getting your hands dirty, then a cleaning service might just be your perfect business. There is a variety of opportunities in professional cleaning and the income is good.
If you have multiple accounts and lose one client, you only lose part of your income and can usually pick up another client easily.

The cleaning industry has two primary market groups: consumer and commercial. The consumer market consists primarily of residential maid services, carpet cleaners, window cleaners and a variety of other cleaning services. The commercial market is dominated by janitorial services providing a wider range of services. You can serve multiple markets or pick a niche.   You can build an extremely profitable business that will generate revenue very quickly on a part-time or full-time basis. There will be no zoning problems since you will be going to your customer's location. If you want to do the work yourself, you can stay small but service more clients with hired help. A partner or family member may be able to help with the work.

If you like working outside, the opportunities in niche areas such as window cleaning and pressure washing are abundant. Residential maid services offer predictable hours while disaster restoration and cleanup can mean calls at all hours of the day or night. If you choose to do residential maid services, choose upscale homes that are more expensive as your target area since they will pay better.

Skills

The niche you choose will determine what skills you need. One of the most critical requirements for you and your employees or partners is honesty. Clients must be able to trust you in their home or business. Insure and bond your business. A maid service is the simplest business and requires the least amount of equipment and skill. Many times the homeowner will want you to use their equipment such as mops and vacuums. A commercial janitorial service will require training on the use of special equipment and cleaning solutions.

Equipment

Order your cleaning equipment and supplies through a local supplier. Establish a wholesale account to save money on your cleaning supplies.

Another niche is to advertise an "all natural" cleaning service for those who want no chemicals. A growing league of consumers are wanting to use more natural solutions without the chemicals and artificial fragrances. Not only are some of these chemicals dangerous, but also bad for your health as a cleaning professional. This brings us to the issue of whether you want to subject yourself to a barrage of chemicals. Change the cleaners you are using or wear protective gear when you know you are using something dangerous especially when used repeatedly.

- Vacuum
- Mops
- Dusters
- Buffer
- Steam cleaner
- Carpet cleaner
- Squeegee
- Rags
- Cleaning solutions

Income

Cleaning service businesses earn from $50,000 to $90,000 a year. If you are on the east or west coast in a larger city, earnings tend be higher. There are good opportunities in outlying areas and smaller towns where there is little competition.

Make business cards and flyers with your services listed. After you get your first few clients, word of mouth will be one of your best advertisements. Give cards to local real estate agents, rental agencies, and advertise in your local paper and on Craig's List.

Associations

Association of Residential Cleaning Services International - http://www.arcsi.org/

National Cleaning Association - http://www.nationalcleaningassociation.com/

Mobile Detail Unit

A mobile detail business does not require a large amount of start-up capital, and can earn a very good income. Auto detail operations travel to the customer's location to clean and detail cars, trucks, RVs, and possibly even tractors. If you have a truck or van, a mobile detail company can be started for under $2,000.

A mobile detail business provides car-detailing services such as cleaning, waxing and buffing. Unlike a stationary location, mobile detailing units allow business owners to work at the homes and businesses of customers. A detail business typically charges a set fee for each type of service.

Skills

Detailing cars as a profession is demanding work, however, it keeps you in good physical shape. There is a difference between amateur and professional auto detailing.

Equipment

The equipment used to clean your own car will not last long when used commercially. Buy a high quality rotary buffer. They are not as easy to use as a home orbital buffer and can damage the paint if you are not careful. Get training on the use of the rotary buffer before using it on an expensive car. Practice using junk cars before attempting to work on a customer's car. Your efficiency will be greatly improved with professional tools.

Equipment

- Water tank
- Pressure washer
- Hose w/ hose reel

- Hose wand
- Soft water system
- Canopies
- Carpet extractor
- Steamer
- Vacuum
- Generator
- Towels
- Brush /misc. small tools
- Extension cords
- Shelves
- Detail supplies (soap, polish, degreaser, etc....)
- Buffers/polishers
- Stepladders
- Wastewater reclaim system
- Wastewater holding tank
- Laptop computer
- GPS system

Small Tools

- White wool cutting pad
- Poly Wool cutting pad
- Foam cutting pad
- Foam polishing/finishing pad
- Wheel brush
- Spoke brush
- Nylon scrub brush
- Spoke brush
- Detail brush
- Car wash mitts
- Three colors of towels - chemical & grease; water & wax; glass (wash separately)

Detail Supplies

- Car Wash shampoo
- Engine degreaser
- Wheel cleaner (non-acid)
- All purpose cleaner
- Tar & Grease remover
- Extractor shampoo
- Carpet & upholstery shampoo
- Glass cleaner
- Leather conditioner
- Dressing (water-based only for engines, tires & interiors)
- 800 Grit Heavy Compound
- 1200 Grit Medium Compound
- 2000 Grit Light Compound
- Micro fine Compound
- Swirl Remover/Polish
- Paint Sealant or Wax (paint sealant is better)

Start out by going to customer's homes and detail at their location. Most detailers carry their own water supply. A tarp may be needed to shade the vehicle from the sun. Dress nicely and look neat. People will judge whether you can make their car or truck look beautiful initially by the way you appear. Walk around the customer's car and point out any problems in the condition of the paint and how you could correct the problem. They may need a dent repair that you can refer to someone you know. A small referral fee may be arranged for passing on the work. Consider offering a maintenance program that will include washing once a week and waxing once or twice a month for a set price. Have an agreement form with you and collect the check up front. You will have a steady customer.

Your best area while looking for work is high-end cars and neighborhoods. It is easier to sell your services on more expensive cars. You may find work from used car dealers, although they do not pay well. Dealers do have large amounts of steady work.

Carrying general liability insurance and a form of garage-keepers coverage not only provides protection for you and your cliental, but also shows potential customers that you are professional. Get coverage that will cover the type of vehicles you will be working on. Insure your detail rig as well.

Income

A mobile detail business generates an average of between $50 and $100 an hour. A full-time mobile detail business can make over $75,000 in profits each year allowing for approximately three months off for bad weather, marketing time, and a vacation. Have a simple price list for customers to avoid overwhelming them with choices.

Several factors can affect the actual amount of money made by a mobile detail unit. Weather can influence the number of customers requiring detailing services. During a month of high rain or freezing weather, for instance, the demand for car washing may decrease and income can be significantly reduced. A detail business can also increase income by offering extra services. Some detail businesses offer dent removal or windshield repair, in addition to basic detailing.

If you live in a farming/ranching community, a great place to find business is a farm. They can keep you busy all day with cars, trucks, and tractors. Generally, farmers do not have the time to do these types of chores, especially during their busy season. You can advertise in Craig's List for free, local newspapers, and advertise yourself with a big sign on the van or truck. This industry is growing, and income for mobile detail units has the potential to increase significantly.

Mobile Food Truck

Mobile kitchens, also known as catering and food trucks, are a type of food business that operates by going to different locations. Various types of food, from ice cream to sandwiches, are sold by mobile food kitchens. The start-up expenses on a mobile food truck are much lower and less risky than a restaurant. The food trucks are seen in many places at special events such as auctions, fairs, etc. Ideal stopping points for a catering truck route include construction sites, factories, parks, beaches and sporting events. Trailers are used in many cases. A vendor can unhook the trailer and still have a vehicle to use. The trailer can also be set up several days in advance where another vehicle would be required if you had to leave a mobile truck on site.

There are two types of catering trucks: hot trucks, such as Mobile Food Preparation Vehicles (MFPV), which allow food to be prepared as customers order; and cold trucks, such as Industrial Catering Vehicles (ICV), which sell only prepackaged foods. The hot trucks have a driver and one more person, who may be a family member. The hot truck will need a minimum of one cook and one server. Cold trucks only need a driver who is usually the server and money collector since it is a self-service vehicle.

Skills

Sell a specific type of food. The space for cooking and selling will be quite small, so you should specialize in a specific variety of food. For instance, you can sell cupcakes, tacos, gourmet hot dogs, crepes or burgers. Sell items that can be eaten without sitting down.

Contact your state's department of health to determine what permits and certifications are needed to legally operate a mobile kitchen. They can also tell you which areas in town you will be allowed to sell. A tax permit and food handler permit may be required and your truck or trailer may have to be inspected.

Equipment

Most mobile kitchens are large trucks but I have seen a number of mobile kitchens set up in used remodeled camping trailers or special food trailers. Buy wholesale napkins, cups, plates, and utensils instead of paying retail.

- Truck or Trailer
- Cooking Equipment
- Cooling Equipment
- Generator

Income

There is no average salary listing for this business. This type of business will be largely cash intensive, since most individuals purchasing items from a mobile vendor pay in cash. There is a markup percentage of about 100% on cold foods and about 200% on hot foods. For example, if an item is purchased for $0.50, it will generally sell for $1 or more. If you served 200 people at an event and the average ticket was $8.00 per person, the gross income would be $1,600. An estimate of the net income might be $1,000. Some items are marked up by 100% and others 200%.   Earn extra revenue year-round by vending at city fairs, carnivals, car shows, flea markets, and farmers markets.

Mobile Notary Public

Despite technological advances, documents such as property deeds, wills and loan papers still require an official signature and stamp by a notary. Most banks and real estate offices have a notary, but the current trend is using notaries who come to your home or business on call. In today's busy world, the mobile notary business is in demand. Your client will appreciate the fact that they do not have to take time off work or drive miles to get a document notarized. The mobile notary goes to the client's office or home.

Skills

Setting up this kind of business has strict rules. Most states require completion of a course, passing an exam, and all require a state license. Check with your state for regulations and costs, and visit the National Notary Association for materials and more information. It is important to put out the word to friends, family and co-workers about your new notary business. Documents you could process include Lender's Loan Documents, Real Estate Deeds, Powers of Attorney and Living Trusts.

Equipment

Set up a professional website with search engine optimization in order for your business to be found locally. Pick a niche and market locally.   Your equipment is minimal.

- Car/vehicle
- Computer
- Printer
- Website
- Notary stamp

Income

The average mobile notary earns from $31,000 to $69,000 a year. Your location will dictate how much you will earn. A large city will give you the best opportunity to make a higher income. As a mobile notary, your costs are low and there are fringe benefits. You can drive around, meet interesting people and charge a premium for providing door-to-door service. Travel fees are charged in addition to the standard notary charge of $10 per signature.

Sample rates for a notary who advertises online and specializes in real estate is included below.

- Regular loan package $155.
- Single document $75.
- In house sign-up (documents already at escrow or client) $105

They charge a $35 travel fee plus $10 per notarized signature if the client has documents. If the travel range exceeds 15 miles or your set limit, have the client call for a quote. You may need to increase travel charges since the price of gas has increased dramatically.

Associations

National Notary Association - http://nationalnotary.org/

Moving Service

The average family moves once every five years. The decision to start a moving service requires a lot of preparation. Almost everyone needs help moving and sometimes friends and family are not available to help. Residential and commercial moving services can be a lucrative business. Try starting out small with moves around town and for single items. Many people buy an item and cannot move it by themselves or do not have a truck.

Skills

If you plan to do the moving work yourself, be sure you are physically up to the challenge. Helping someone move is entirely different than moving one or two houses a day. At least one additional person is needed to help lift heavy items.

Equipment

Some states require moving companies to obtain licenses and permits. Requirements vary by state. A test may even be required in some locations. Have a damage and liability insurance policy. No matter how careful you are, accidents will happen. You may be selected for a job instead of another company simply because your company has insurance.

- Truck
- Trailer
- Ramp
- Tie downs
- Dollies
- Straps
- DOT sticker
- Permits
- License
- Boxes
- Packaging materials
- Website

Income

A small mover will charge from $50 to $200 to move an item. The charges depend on the size and the miles. More items would add to the cost. Research what movers are charging in your area. Charge extra for boxes and packing materials. If you start small with a pickup and a trailer, be sure to buy insurance.

Associations

American Moving and Storage Association - http://www.promover.org/

Paintless Dent Removal

There are millions of cars on the road and many have small dents. Paintless Dent Removal (PDR) is an innovative, economical, fast, and effective method of repairing minor damage. Almost instant repair can be done while your customer waits. I can personally attest to how well this business works since I just had my truck repaired using PDR. I made an appointment with a local body shop, they called their favorite PDR man, and he fixed the dent in my truck door panel in less than an hour. The work was perfect. The bid to take the door apart, fix the dent, and repaint was $400 so the $125 was a bargain and I did not have to leave my truck. There is no painting, it is environmentally friendly, costs about one third of the traditional auto body method, and there are no consumables. Most dents only take 15 minutes to repair but mine was one of the worst that could be fixed with PDR.

Skills

Training will be required to learn how to use the PDR tools. A number of companies offer training and the tools can be bought online. The more experience you get, the faster a job can be completed. That means more jobs could be done in a day.

Make business cards and flyers. You may want to work with some body shops. You would pay them a referral fee and collect the rest. The body shop may price their work too high and the customer would be without their car at least two days. Many people would choose to drive the car with the dent. The customer would pay $100 to $125 versus $350 to $400. This price difference creates a huge opportunity for the PDR business.

Pass out business cards and leave flyers listing your services and prices with some of the businesses listed below. You may have a price range from small dents to larger dents. Advertise in your local paper, the yellow pages, and Craig's List.

Potential markets are listed below.

- Private vehicles
- Car dealers
- Car rentals
- Body shop
- Panel shops
- Insurance companies
- Fleet vehicles
- Car auctions

Equipment

Special tools are needed for this business. A set of PDR tools costs from $1,500 to $3,000. A van is the perfect vehicle for this business since you need to protect your tools and they should be easy to load and unload.

- Van
- PDR tool set
- Lights and reflectors
- Suction cups and straps
- Rolling work seat

Income

The income opportunity for PDR is great.   The average price is $100 per dent, which takes 15 minutes to repair. Difficult dents are $125 to $150 and take up to an hour. If you repair two dents per day at $100 each, you will make $200 a day or $1000 a week. Using 50 workweeks your income would be $50,000 a year. An increase to repairing four dents per day would make $100,000. Your actual work hours would be less than four hours per day not counting travel time.

Associations

National Paintless Dent Removal Association - http://npdra.org/

Personal Shopper

For many busy working people, time is money. They do not have time to take off work to go pick out a gift for a birthday or wedding. Picking up the dry cleaning and shopping is time consuming. Others who use a personal shopper are those who are not able to shop. Either they cannot drive, are disabled, or not able to walk very far. Busy executives, salespeople and small business owners can use the services of a personal shopper.

Skills

Good taste is an important asset for the personal shopper business. Picking an appropriate gift and card for your customer's intended event and person is an important talent. Seniors are in need of shopping services since many are not able to shop themselves.

Equipment

The only equipment needed for this business is dependable transportation. If you are shopping for several people at a time, you may need a car with a lot of room such as a station wagon, SUV, or van. If you are carrying many packages, a rolling cart may save trips from the car to the home.

Pass out business cards and flyers listing your services. Post your cards or flyer on bulletin boards. Word of mouth is a big advertisement for this service. You may even take people to doctor's appointments.

Income

Personal shoppers earn from $25,000 to $55,000 a year. Call other personal shoppers in your area and get their rates. You can charge a commission on purchases, fee for each order, and mileage. If you have to wait for someone that you have taken to an appointment, that time should also be billed. Often elderly people will ask you to do a few extra things, like changing light bulbs, and do not mind paying extra for other simple services. A personal shopper can be a gratifying business since people are very appreciative.

Personal Trainer

If you are a fitness buff or avid runner, you may be able to make a living by teaching others what you have learned. Many people's New Year's resolution is to lose weight, and many of them are looking for professional help to shed the unwanted pounds and get in better physical shape. People look for a personal trainer to ensure they do not do exercises that will hurt them. There is no real age limit for this business since some have not started their business until in their 50's and 60's.

Skills

The first step in starting a fitness business is to become certified as a personal trainer. After you are certified, you could work in a gym to gain experience and start your own business on the side. Make sure you are being ethical and do not try to steal business from your employer. Your employment may forbid work on the side in personal training while working at their gym. You may need to quit and start your own business. Many of your clients from the gym will probably follow you.

One of your best advertisements besides word of mouth is your own story with before and after pictures. You can specialize in a certain area such as working with clients 50 plus, people recovering from injuries, weight lifting, weight loss, Pilates, or yoga.

Equipment

Find clients by getting to know people at the gym you already attend. Ask your gym about becoming a trainer on staff to learn the business. Talk to friends, relatives, and colleagues who either do not have time to go to a gym or feel embarrassed in a room full of people running on treadmills. You may need some basic equipment such as a portable CD player, mats, and an exercise ball.

Income

The income for a personal trainer ranges from $42,000 to $67,000.

Associations

Aerobics and Fitness Association of America - http://www.afaa.com/
National Personal Training Institute of Colorado - http://www.nptitrainer.com/
National Academy of Sports Medicine - http://www.nasm.org/
National Council on Strength and Fitness - http://www.ncsf.org/
National Strength and Conditioning Association - http://www.nsca-lift.org/

Pet Groomer

Mobile pet groomers wash, comb, clip and style dogs' coats according to the characteristics of the breed and the owner's wishes.   The work is normally done in the groomers van, which is parked outside of the owner's home. The demand is rising for pet groomers.

Skills

Training in grooming procedures is necessary. You may go to a grooming school or learn from another groomer. The groomer has to know what type of cut is correct for which breed. The groomer must have the physical strength to lift the dogs into tubs and on grooming tables. Your mobile van will probably be equipped with ramps into the wash area and on the drying and grooming table but there will be unwilling dogs that need some help. The groomer needs to know how to handle problem dogs without hurting the dog or themselves. You will need to have a true love for animals.

Equipment

A mobile pet groomer business requires a custom van and all of the tools related to grooming. Your business should be completely self-contained in a van or other suitable enclosed vehicle.

- Customized Van with water supply and generator
- Driers
- Clippers
- Small grooming tools
- Shampoo and conditioner
- Bows and decorations

Income

The yearly income for a pet groomer ranges from $22,000 to $32,000. The income is dependent on location and clients. This is not a get rich quick business but if it is your passion, it might be perfect for you.

Associations

National Dog Groomers Association - http://www.nationaldoggroomers.com/
National Association of Professional Creative Groomers - http://thenapcg.com/

Photographer

Since the advent of SLR digital cameras, the photography business has declined in some areas such as studios. Now, anyone with the right camera equipment and skills can set up a home photography business. The success of your business will depend on your camera expertise and marketing skills. The business is now highly competitive but there are still niches where you can succeed in photography. You need to be serious about photography and find your niche in the business. You may need to find several specialties. For instance, in some locations, wedding photography and family portrait photography is fairly saturated.

Skills

Knowing how to use your camera is imperative. You must be able to compose an attractive picture and know how to use lighting. Almost all photography is edited now with software. You need to be competent at using several different types of photo software. If you do not already have the camera and software skills, there are many classes and groups where you can gain information.

Try this business on a part-time basis. The market has widened but the price has fallen.

Equipment

Below is a list of equipment needed for a photography business. Other items may be needed depending on the type of photography you choose. If you choose sports photography, you will need different equipment than wedding photography. Professional camera equipment is expensive but you can buy the basics and add more lenses and lights later. When you decide this is the business for you and make some money, acquire a backup camera, especially for special events.

- Pro or Semi Pro SLR digital camera

- Set of lenses for your niche
- Editing software—Adobe Photoshop or Corel PaintShop Photo Pro
- Portable lighting equipment
- Camera cases
- Tripod/monopod
- Computer
- Photo quality monitor
- Printer
- Website

Business cards are very important in this business. If you do a shoot at a sporting event, you will need to hand out your card to everyone in order for people to find your website and buy pictures of themselves or family members. An outgoing friendly personality will help you get more work. A website is needed for display and sales of your work. If you do sports photography, you will sell from that site. Some of the programs you can join offer your own mini website; they will fulfill orders and ship directly to your customer. Most of them offer photos on paper, canvas, and a long list of gift items such as cups, aprons, puzzles, key chains and more.

Listed below are some areas you can consider.

- Fine art
- Stock
- Sports
- Wedding
- Event
- Portrait
- Book covers
- Greeting cards
- Advertising
- Real estate
- Tourism

- Travel
- Press

Income

The average income for a photographer is $24,000 to $70,000. Marketing skills will need to be good to reach the upper income levels. Research your competition and price accordingly. It helps to find niches that need filled and add them to your list of services.

Associations

Professional Photographers of America - http://www.ppa.com/
National Press Photographers - http://www.nppa.org/
North American Nature Photography Association - http://www.nanpa.org/
The Association of Photographers - http://home.the-aop.org/

Plant Leasing

A plant leasing business rents plants to businesses and furnishes care for the plants for a set or ongoing length of time. Companies do not have the time, staff, or talent to take care of the plants, much less to water them. Many offices have a stark look. A plant leasing service can achieve a lush classy image instantly. The service will maintain that lush classy image. If any plants do not look good, the service replaces the plants as part of the lease.

The economy has hurt this business and some people are getting price conscious. Many businesses are doing well and those are the ones to target for plant leasing.

Skills

This business uses no more than 15 to 16 different types of plants so you will not have to be a nursery specialist. Learn about the plants you will offer for lease and know how to care for them, their watering schedule and fertilization. Do not mix plants with different watering schedules to avoid additional trips for maintenance. Plan on maintenance and watering every 7 to 10 days. Plant leasing is physically demanding and you will need to climb a ladder to work on high plants. You will need to be a people person to visit with people about your business and get accounts.

Buy only the plants needed for each location based on a signed contract. Select varieties that will be on the same watering schedule. Many wholesalers will deliver. Each multistory building could contain 50 or more potential clients.

Below is a list of potential clients.

- Building lobbies
- Car dealerships
- Hotels
- Retirement homes
- Banks
- Property managers
- Financial institutions
- Restaurants
- Engineering firms
- Architects
- Insurance firms
- Corporate offices
- Beauty shops
- Day spas
- Fitness centers
- Surgical centers
- Medical facilities
- Hospitals
- Dentists

Equipment

Since a delivery vehicle is only needed for the day of delivery, you may want to rent by the day. Owning your own delivery vehicle is handy if you have a number of accounts. A dolly will be needed to deliver and move the plants since they will be heavy. This is a physical job so you should be in good shape, able to carry water containers, and not afraid of climbing ladders.

- Van or truck (can rent for delivery day only)
- Dolly
- Ladder
- . Pruning shears
- Water can

Estimate costs and what you will need to spend on each contract. Fixed costs would include licenses and permits, fuel, insurance, phone, office supplies, internet connection, etc. Include the cost of plants and plant replacements, as you need to replace the original plants. Replacement time is normally every three years. The amount of light in the building will have a lot to do with how long your plants look good. Keep them fresh and good looking since your plants are your advertisement. Do not skimp on the quality of plants you furnish.   Other costs include shipping, supplies, decorative containers, maintenance, and labor for the maintenance period, and bookkeeping. You will begin with a contract with your client for the number of plants including care for a minimum non-cancellable lease term. Terms can be defined for the agreement to continue for the same price or a renegotiated price after the initial lease expires.

Define your service boundaries, find a good wholesale plant source, make a list of plants you will carry, service instructions for each type of plant, list of target markets, and your price sheet. Take pictures of each plant species you will carry and take pictures of each client's plant display. Pictures of containers to match themes for the space you are filling and surrounding area.

Purchase top quality plants. It is tempting to save money and purchase lower-priced plants but remember that your plants are the advertisements for your business. Look for plant wholesalers in your area.

Look sharp when you go in every week for maintenance and watering. A uniform or nice apron with your company name embroidered on the front turns you into a walking advertisement and you may get more business that way. Always carry business cards and brochures or fliers. You will want to have a portfolio with photos of your plants. People will imagine how those plants would look in their facility. Study designs with different plants and containers to make creative designs.

Income

The minimum contract would be about $100 a month and your maximum could be as large as $2500 per month. Presenting your self in a professional manner will get you top dollar on your contract prices. You can start this business part time and it should replace your full-time job by the time you get 10 to 14 contracts.

Associations

Interior Scape - http://www.interiorscape.com/ Forum for Plantscape Professionals

Pressure Washing

Pressure washing can be a very lucrative business. Homes in many parts of the country have to be pressure washed every year due to humid conditions where mold starts to take over. Pressure washers can clean concrete, wood, metal, and even roofs. Homes should be pressure washed before painting.

There is a demand for pressure washing, and it is possible to make upwards of $80 per hour.   It is very important to start out on the right foot, by buying quality equipment and establishing a customer base. Rent a pressure washer at your local building supply and try several washers before deciding which model to buy. Always dress neatly and look professional.

Skills

Become competent using the pressure washer you purchase. It is easy to damage a home with a pressure washer that is turned up too high. Practice on many different surfaces to avoid damaging a customer's property. Market your services to the following clients.

- Homes
- Decks
- Businesses
- Driveways
- Colleges
- Pools
- Tile roofs
- Brick buildings and walls
- Tennis courts
- Toll booths
- Gas stations
- Farms
- Stables
- Livestock facilities
- Poultry facilities
- Platforms
- Silos

Equipment

A truck, van or trailer is needed to carry the pressure washer. Research any chemicals that you need for specific jobs. There are websites that carry everything for the pressure washing trade. Place business cards and flyers on local bulletin boards. Advertise in your local paper and in Craig's List. Below is a list of minimum equipment needed.

- Truck, Van, or Trailer
- Pressure washer
- Nozzles
- Extension wand
- 100 feet of ¾ inch premium quality water hose
- Misc. accessories

Income

There is not an actual listing for pressure washing income. The average charge per hour is from $70 to $120 per hour. Expenses for your vehicle, pressure washer, and supplies must be subtracted along with a home office, computer, invoices, cards, ads, etc.

Associations

Power Washers of North America - http://www.thepwna.org/

Professional Organizer

Professional organizing is a perfect business for people with a knack for neatness and arrangement. Clutter in a workspace or living space can create a high level of stress. The professional organizing industry has grown steadily as people try to gain better control of their lives. People with more demands and less free time are struggling to manage their life and clean up the clutter building up

in their lives. Many are turning to professional organizers for help.
With growing consumer demand, there are many business
opportunities for professional organizers.

Skills

Along with natural organizing skills, read and train yourself about
the art of organizing. There are many books in the market on
organizing. Training and certification are available through such
organizations as The Board of Certification for Professional
Organizers listed below. Certification is not necessary in this
business, but voluntary. Listed below are some of the skills a
professional organizer will need.

- Understand what a client wants
- Customize the organization to client's needs
- Visualize the big picture
- Customize organizational systems to meet client needs
- Ability to teach basic organizing skills
- Break goals down into manageable steps
- Categorize and plan ahead
- Use technology to support organizing efforts
- Physical and mental endurance
- Compassion
- Responsibility
- Professionalism

Equipment

There is no equipment needed for this business other than a
dependable vehicle. If you expand your services to include closet
organizers, you will need basic tools to put the organizers together
and a truck to haul the organizer, unless they are being delivered. If
the organization is complicated, a laptop may be needed with
building software allowing room dimensions and furniture to show
on the screen.

Make professional business card and flyers/brochures. Market your services on the radio, your local newspaper, or Craig's List. Leave business cards and flyers in grocery stores in affluent neighborhoods. You may want to send mailings to a specific zip code. Word of mouth will be your best advertisement, once your business has a number of satisfied clients. Be sure to carry insurance to protect your business. Customers are more likely to hire contractors with insurance.

Income

The income range of a professional organizer is $20,000 to $50,000 a year. You can charge hourly or set half-day and full-day flat rates for your time. Since all clutter organization is the same, it is a good idea to choose an area of specialization. You may want to specialize in cleaning out garages, busy professionals, offices, closets or whole houses. Tour the space that needs organizing before estimating the time needed to complete the job.

Associations

National Association of Professional Organizers - http://www.napo.net/

Screen Repair & Installation

This business is great for people who do not have time to take their screens off and haul them to a store to be repaired. They have to make a second trip to pick them up and then install the repaired screens. Millions of window and door screens are repaired or replaced every year. Your customers will be happy that you can fix their screens on the spot.

Skills

Learn the best and fastest ways to replace screens and practice. Screens are not high tech and not hard to learn how to replace. Call your local screen repair service companies and see how much they are charging. This will give you an idea of what the rates are. Add the cost of your mileage and more for your customer's convenience.

Learn how to manufacture new screen frames in your van or trailer. Frames are built using heavy-duty gauge aluminum framing and heavy-duty fabric. Screen frames of today come in a variety of colors and sizes depending on the application.

Equipment

This business requires minimal basic tools and materials. An enclosed truck or van is needed to provide protection from the weather. Make cards and flyers with your services and service area listed. Advertise in local papers, Craig's List, and on local bulletin boards. Word of mouth will travel fast if you do a competent job. Offer a commission for jobs sent to you by house painters, window cleaners, and landscapers. Contact residential and commercial property management firms, apartment building managers, community associations, schools, government agencies and local businesses.

- Van or Trailer
- Miter saw
- Screen rollers
- Screen materials
- Screen replacement parts
- Frame materials

Income

A well-established mobile screen business can generate sales in excess of $100,000 a year. Your location will dictate your income potential. The cost of the materials is inexpensive and is marked up five to eight times.

Videographer

If you love to record everything from events to life in general and have talent making videos, this business may be the one for you. A professional videographer records events such as weddings, sports, parties, meetings, courses, presentations, public events etc. You will use a professional quality video camera, edit the recording, and produce copies of the video on CDs and DVDs. This business may also be combined with professional photography but you cannot run both cameras simultaneously. You may be able to take videos in one time interval of your event and pictures in another, or hire a photographer to help with your event. A videographer is not necessarily skilled at still photography.

Skills

While anyone can pick up a camcorder today and start recording, a professional videographer adds creativity, skills and knowledge to produce a high quality professional video. Videos are important for once in a lifetime events such as weddings and sporting events.

A professional videographer must have editing skills essential to create a quality visual presentation. When editing a video you will fix errors in the video and audio recording, delete unnecessary parts of the video, add transition effects during scene changes, and possibly add music. When the editing is complete, burn the final copies on CDs or DVDs for delivery to the client.

Equipment

The following equipment will be needed to start a videographer business. Since live events only afford one chance for a video, carry backup equipment and batteries.

- Professional Digital Video Camera
- Computer
- Video editing software such as Adobe Premiere Pro or iMovie
- CD/DVD burning software to create copies of video
- Copyright free music
- External microphones
- Video lights

You will be recording events according to your client's time schedule and location. This involves traveling to the client's specified location with your equipment, setting up the equipment, and recording the video. Try to gather details about the event including the location, important people in the event, ceremonies, or special parts of the event, and time frames.

It is advisable to visit the location of the event and check out any rules related to permitted areas for recording, bright lighting, usage of microphones etc. Locate the electrical outlets for lighting equipment if needed.   Most equipment runs on batteries with the exception of some lighting. Make sure your batteries are charged and that you have spares.

While there are no specific legal and insurance requirements that apply to the videographer business, be aware of copyright restrictions for recording a live event such as a stage show. Make sure you have insurance to protect against loss, theft or damage to your expensive video equipment.

Set up a website listing all of the events you are willing to video. List previous clients, with permission, and get testimonials to put on your website. Make professional quality business cards and brochures. List ads in newspapers and list your business in local directories. Contact banquet halls, wedding planners, and event managers.

Prospective clients will want proof of your capabilities and skills. Build a portfolio of your past work to show potential clients. Word of mouth from satisfied customers is one of your best advertisements.

Income

Videographer income ranges from $25,000 to $104,000 a year. The average income is $56,000 a year. Usually the services of a videographer are offered for a set price that includes recording, editing and producing the final video. This should, however, be based on the length of the event to be covered. Charge extra for longer events. Include the cost of travel, transportation of your equipment, and creating multiple copies in the price of the package. Fees range from $250 to $1,000 a day. Most events last an hour or two.

Associations

National Professional Videographers Association (NPVA) -- http://npva.org/
Wedding & Event Videographers Association (WEVA) -- http://www.weva.com/public_web/
National Association of Professional Wedding Videographers (NAPWV) -- http://www.napwv.com/

Windshield Repair

The windshield repair business is very popular. It is much less expensive to have a chip or crack repaired rather than have a windshield replaced. Many people do not want to turn in a claim to their insurance company so having a windshield repaired is the perfect solution. It takes 15 minutes or less to repair a windshield. Insurance companies are happy to pay for the much smaller cost of repair rather than replacement.

Windshields are the number one insurance claim in the United States. The windshield repair business grosses over one billion dollars a year. Since windshield replacement is expensive, more businesses and individuals are turning to windshield glass repair versus replacement. Typical clients of windshield repair are listed below.

- Individuals
- Fleets
- Insurance companies
- Car lots
- Car rental companies
- Businesses using vehicles

Skills

Training is the key to success in this business. A number of companies offer training and supplies. I would suggest hands on training versus watching a video and trying to find cars to practice repairing. Do research checking these online companies. Call the companies that look the best, order their information, and talk to their sales people. Check on their training, how long they have been in business and if their system can repair not only chips but also cracks. I have an acquaintance that repairs windshields and does very well. He sits in his SUV in an empty lot between a bank and a restaurant on a busy street. He has a large folding sign he sets out by his vehicle. One key thing that sets him above the competition, other than being skilled, is he is there rain or shine so people know he will be there consistently, other than during snowstorms. He sits there all day and sometimes has three cars lined up waiting.

Equipment

The tools for this business are minimal. A small stepladder is needed to reach the higher truck windshields. The specialized windshield repair tools will fit in a small toolbox the size of a fishing tackle box. The cost for initial training and supplies is anywhere from $1,500 to $2,500. After the initial training and tools, supplies are not very expensive.

Income

Auto window repair is very profitable. The average repair of a stone break retails for $50-60.00 and a long crack $90-150.00. The cost for supplies for the typical repair is less than one dollar.

Associations

National Windshield Repair Association - http://www.nwrassn.org/

NOTE: Please refer to my websites for business resources, books, courses, software, equipment and supplies for the businesses in this book.   From time to time additional business opportunities will be posted on my website. I hope this information makes the research for your new business easier. Clicking on the links in the websites will take you to resources for each item.

http://www.pdsloss.com/
http://www.RealisticHomeBusinesses.com/

Chapter 11

In Your Home

Adult Residential Foster Care Givers

Adult foster care homes provide room, board and general supervision of personal care services in a private residence. The private residence is typically in the caregiver's home but might be the individual's home. An adult foster care home can be more affordable than other care facilities and care is provided in a home setting. Care and supervision are provided to maintain a safe and secure setting around the clock. Adult foster care can meet the needs of adults who require periodic or regular assistance with activities of daily living, but do not require nursing services. Examples of "activities of daily living" include: dressing, bathing, eating, brushing teeth, and combing hair.

Skills/Services

Adult foster care homes may serve both private-pay and state-pay individuals. The Department of Social Services is responsible for case management services to individuals age 60 and over and receiving state payment. If the individual is under the age of 60, normally the Department of Human Services' Division of Developmental Disabilities is responsible for payment and case management. Check with your county and state for their regulations.

Owners or operators of adult foster care homes may require additional staff to assist with duties. Adult care can be very hard and tiring. Remember in most cases, adults live in your home and need care 24 hours a day, 7 days a week.

Individuals Appropriate for Adult Foster Care
- Oriented to time, person and place and not a danger to themselves or others in the adult foster care home
- Unable to live independently
- Require minimal supervision and/or assistance in completing one or more of the following: dressing, personal hygiene, transportation, ambulation, nutrition, health supervision
- Capable of taking action for self-preservation in case of fire or storm with direction
- Usually has control of bowel and bladder, but may have stress incontinence and/or capable of meeting their own needs when incontinent

Individuals Not Appropriate for Adult Foster Care
- Consistently not oriented to time, person and place to such a degree they pose a danger to themselves or others in the home
- Unable or unwilling to meet own personal hygiene needs under minimal supervision
- Has a communicable disease or infectious condition which pose a threat to the health or safety of other residents of the home
- Chronically disruptive and unable or unwilling to comply with adult foster care rules
- Behavior poses a threat to other residents
- Unable to self-medicate on one's own or with the assistance of supervision or monitoring
- Require a complex, therapeutic diet
- Require any other type of care which can only be provided safely by or under the supervision of a licensed practical nurse or a registered nurse

Services

Adult Foster Care providers must provide the following services and items:

- Shelter
- At least three meals a day
- Assistance with personal care,
- Companionship
- Assistance with activities of daily living
- Expendable items used by the clients in small quantities such as facial and toilet tissue and personal items such as towels and soap, laundry services, non-medical transportation and socialization

This type of business also complicates the distinction between consultant and employee. All of the requirements of an independent contractor must be met if you want to be considered a consultant instead of employee.

Consultants operate under their own business name and license/certificate. Consultants are free to decline work and are not subject to work place policies and supervision. While you may work as a consultant or employee, the tax benefits are usually greater for consultants.

Licensing and Certification—Colorado Example

You must meet the state or city regulations and inspections when taking care of individuals for your city, county, or state. The State of Colorado classifies facilities which provide overnight and room and board for 1 or 2 residents in private homes as Elderly Care Group Homes. (A more common term for this is "Adult Foster Care Home".) Check with your state and/or county for the regulations for adult foster care.

The Colorado Department of Health Care Policy and Financing's Long Term Care and Support Services Division has empowered each Colorado county to certify and license Elderly Care Group Homes; not all counties participate in this program.

Workers' compensation law allows an exemption for an employee performing adult foster care duties of assistance to the residents of an adult foster home licensed for five or fewer adults where room, board, and 24-hour care is provided.

Income

Pay for this work can be very good, especially when taking care of several individuals but make sure this is something you really want to take on. The stress of 24 hours a day, 7 days a week care can be overwhelming. The average pay per day is $75 to $80. Other statistics range from $29,000 to $33,000 a year. This is the pay for one person. Taking care of two or three individuals would significantly increase your income.

Employment for personal and home care aides is expected to grow by 46 percent through the year 2018. Job growth will be spurred largely by an aging population's need for health care services.

Bed & Breakfast

Bed and Breakfasts have become very popular and are becoming even more so lately. Thoughts of a romantic room for two with a crackling fire, beautiful view, fresh coffee and homemade cinnamon rolls come to mind. Bed and Breakfasts are varied in style, such as historic homes, bungalows, schoolhouses, banks, lighthouses, working cattle ranches, dairy farms, waterfront homes and are found in a variety of locations.

A Bed and Breakfast (B&B) business may seem like your dream job. Make sure you are a "people person" before considering this business. You must be committed to working 24 hours a day, 7 days a week, and really enjoy having many different types of personalities and people in your home.

Skills

Your daily routine will require early rising, cooking, cleaning, laundry, shopping, banking, bookkeeping, advertising, marketing, check-ins, check-outs, reservations, and management. Make sure this profession with long hours fits your personality. You cannot leave your office behind in the evenings.

Check local zoning codes carefully since some areas prohibit B&B's. There may be a process you can go through to be approved. Some areas allow rental of two or three rooms with no approval but renting more will require approval and possibly zoning changes. Find out whether there are restrictions on the types of food that can be served, such as a full breakfast versus coffee and muffins. A kitchen inspection and periodic inspections by the health department may be required. Research how you might be affected by the Americans with Disabilities Act. B&B's with more than five rooms must comply with the Americans with Disabilities Act which might greatly increase your home or building renovations.

Equipment

The equipment for this business is mostly a renovated home or building made into guest room and bathrooms. Decide what services and meals you will provide. Some provide only breakfast while others such as cattle ranches, for instance, will furnish all meals since they are normally too far out of town to expect someone to leave for lunch and dinner. Part of the charm of the cattle ranch escape is staying there full time along with the scenery, animals, and experience of the real thing. You will need help in order to get away to shop, go to the bank, and run errands. If your family is part of the operation, you may be able to split the work in order for everyone to have time to themselves and time to attend to personal matters. There should be something alluring about your location or surroundings to draw more customers.

A small B&B generally consists of four to ten guest rooms. The owners interact with customers as if they were invited guests rather than renting a room as in a hotel. Furnish deluxe touches such as baskets of bath and beauty products, chocolates on guest's pillows, iced tea or lemonade on a hot summer afternoon, or coffee and hot chocolate in the winter. Other snacks include a plate of cookies, possibly wine and cheese in the evening, and then of course the home cooked breakfast. Extras are included in the room rate. If guests will not be leaving the property, factor meals and snacks into the rates.

Income

Income is dependent on the area of your B&B, your location, and the services you provide. Based on your location, your nightly rates may also be considerably different from the example. Your nightly rooms may rent at $100 up to $175, especially if activities are included. Be competitive with B&B's in your local area. Before selecting this business, fill in the blanks for your scenario example listed below.

4 rooms at $95 a night
If every room is filled, $380 per day income
$380 times 365 days a year equals $138,700 maximum
Gross income is $138,700 assuming full occupancy every night

The chance of being booked every night of the year is nonexistent no matter where you are located. The average occupancy rate for B&B's in good locations is just over 50%. Your gross income is then cut down to $69,350 with a 50% occupancy. Subtract expenses such as utilities, food, extras, like bath and beauty baskets, and supplies for cleaning, etc., from your gross income to find net income. Do not forget taxes also have to be deducted. This is a lot of hard work and not a get rich quick scheme. It can be a very lucrative business, will pay off your real estate, and pay part of your own living expenses.

Associations

Bed and Breakfast Association --
http://www.bedandbreakfast.com

Child Foster Care—Become a Foster Parent

Helping a child who needs a home is one of the greatest and most unselfish ways you can make a difference in the world. Becoming a foster parent can be a gratifying experience to some, or a grueling ordeal to others.

Foster care is a program, run by your state, which allows stand-in parents, referred to as foster parents, to care for minor children who have been removed from their biological home. There are a number of reasons why children are removed from their biological home, including abuse and neglect. Often, parents who have had their children removed from their home are given a plan to follow, which will result in their regaining custody of their children upon successful completion. The main goal of foster care is to reunite children with their families. It is not uncommon for children placed in foster care to become available for adoption.

Skills

Many of these children have been abused by their parents. Consider your own family. If you have children at home, will they be able to adjust to the changes foster children will bring? You must have time available to devote to caring for the foster children. After caring for these children for months or even years, will you be able to say goodbye to them, possibly to be returned to parents who have abused them in the past?

Foster families do receive compensation from the state but it is far from a get rich quick idea. Caring for these children has to be something that you are dedicated to.

Start by contacting your local department of social services or human services to obtain information about becoming a foster parent. You must to be approved by your state and become part of an agency to be a foster parent. Children are placed by the social services department through agencies. Look in your phone book for the names of foster care agencies in your area. Talk to them about becoming a foster parent. Also talk to some foster parents to get an idea of what the reality of foster care really is.

If you decide to become a foster parent, take the required training and begin the application process. Be prepared for some tough questions about your abilities, motives and lifestyles. Agency workers will inspect your home through both scheduled and unscheduled visits. Be prepared to make the necessary changes to your home to make it safe or appropriate for foster children. You must be at least 21 years old, have adequate financial resources to maintain your home and be able to provide for the child's physical, mental, and character development.

Requirements to become a foster parent may be:
- Background check and finger printing
- Comprehensive home study to ensure child safety
- Classroom hours
- First aid certification
- Medical clearances for all adults and children currently in the home
- Statement proclaiming that corporal punishment will not be used
- Statement advising your role as a mandated reporter

Once you have completed the requirements for your state, you may or may not get a paper copy of your license. Someone from your agency or local child welfare office will contact you to advise you that your home as been approved.

Licensed foster parents usually receive a monthly stipend, mailed from the state or agency. It is not uncommon for parents to spend more than the monthly allotment in order to care for the children. Ensuring your ability to care for children is a very important step when deciding to become licensed.

Depending on the age range you have chosen, you could start getting calls before your license has arrived. The need for qualified foster and foster adoptive homes in the U.S. is great. Taking the steps to become a licensed foster parent is a wonderful way to help children in your state who need a safe place to call home.

The Process

The following description is a sample copy of what the state of Colorado requires for child foster care. Your state may have different steps but this gives you an idea of what is required. Start with your state or county for specific information. Speak to the foster care coordinator in your county department of human or social services or private child placement agencies.

Sample foster care steps (for Colorado)

Step 1: Orientation
Attend an orientation about fostering at the county department or private child placement agency where you choose to pursue the family foster care certification process along with other prospective foster parents. You will learn:

- What foster care means and what your role and responsibilities as a parent will be

- About the children who are placed in out-of-home care, their backgrounds and their ages
- What the certification process involves, such as the application form, the required training classes and the foster family assessment
- How the child's caseworker and the foster care resource caseworkers will work with and support you and your family
- The legal procedures and the assistance and resources available to foster parents
- About permanency, concurrent planning, and situations where children may be placed in the foster home for foster care and later becomes legally free for adoption

Step 2: The Application
The Colorado Department of Human Services Application To Care For Children does not take long to complete, and is free. The county department or private child placement agency where you choose to pursue the family foster care certification will provide an application. A Colorado and national background check for prior criminal and child abuse records will be run on every applicant.

Step 3: Training Classes
Foster parents are required to attend training classes as part of the certification process. The classes are taught by experienced child welfare professionals. In addition to preparing you and your family, the training addresses issues including, legal processes and issues, child growth and development, discipline, parenting and family dynamics. The training also includes the importance of the team approach, working with the birth family, individual differences, as well as the challenges, and the rewards of fostering.

Step 4: Family Assessment
A foster family assessment – also called a "home study" – is the process that helps find appropriate families for the children who are temporarily in out-of-home care. Information is gathered through individual and joint interviews with a caseworker or another

professional that will visit your home. Once your foster family assessment is approved, you may be eligible to have a child placed in your home for foster care.

Here are some of the areas covered in the family assessment:

- Social history, background, personal characteristics, and values
- Problem solving and communication skills
- Parenting skills and family preparation
- Children and other people living in the home
- Family relationships and family support network
- Physical and social environment

Income

State reimbursement per child varies widely per state from $130 to $700 per month. Some states pay by the day. This is not a get rich quick scheme since it sometimes takes more to support a child than what you are paid. You must truly love children to take on being a foster parent.

Home Kitchen

If you enjoy baking and cooking, you may gain both fulfillment and a significant income by starting a home kitchen business. Before you get started, however, it is important to research the laws in your location. Some locations prohibit the selling of goods baked in residential kitchens. If you get a green light, however, a careful plan may help you realize financial success in your home kitchen. In order to make items such as salsa and other cooked goods, a kitchen inspection may be required. You could convert a spare room or small building into a kitchen just for your business. You will have to follow the restrictions in the area where you live and for the type of food you will be creating. Sometimes community kitchens are available to rent that are inspected. Some of the products sold at farmer's markets are prepared in this type of kitchen where large batches of canned or jarred foods can be prepared such as jelly, butters, or salsa. There are some "value added" grants available from the department of agriculture if you raise something such as tomatoes, peppers, wheat, etc. and can make a second product from what you raise.

Types of Home Kitchens

- Catering
- Bakery
- Salsa
- Unusual cookies
- Jelly, Jam, and Butters
- Sell at Farmer's Markets
- Deliver Meals
- Wedding Cakes
- Garlic or Flavored Butters
- Candy
- Ethnic Foods
- Internet Sales
- Jerky
- Concession Stand

Skills/Requirements

Contact the department of licensing and inspections, business regulations office, or health department in your area to learn if operating a food preparation business in your home is legal. Some cities or towns may not allow you to sell food prepared in a home kitchen.

Ask a licensing or health department representative if it is necessary to renovate your home kitchen to begin a baking business. Each city or town may have unique standards for home-based food preparation businesses. Requirements for commercial kitchens include regulations for sink size, counter space and floor space.

Obtain licenses and permits required to run a food preparation business from your home. The requirements vary from location to location, but may include a food handler permit and food preparation license. You will likely have to pay a fee and complete an application to secure the licensing and permits you need. The health department may also inspect your kitchen as part of this process. Apply for a business license if one is required in your city or town. Many locations require all business owners to obtain a license. A business license is typically separate from licensing and permits for preparing and selling food.

Contact your insurance agent to determine the type of insurance that is needed to run a baking/food business out of your home. It is good to have additional liability coverage to protect your business and other assets in the event someone becomes ill or somehow injured by your baked goods.

Create an initial list of goods to sell. You may start out with several baked goods, such as pies, cakes and cookies, and then expand your business to include such things as specialty breads and rolls.

Prepare and price a list of items you will be making. Include the cost of ingredients as well as compensation for your labor. Check out your competition for similar items and price your goods competitively.

Purchase materials for packaging baked goods, such as boxes, Styrofoam or cardboard containers, bags and cellophane. Create labels with the name of your business, contact information, nutritional content and ingredients of the goods you sell. The packaging supplies and labeling methods you choose should meet the guidelines set by the local health department and the Food and

Drug Administration. Indicate whether your items contain nuts or were cooked in a kitchen where nuts were used since a number of people are severely allergic to nuts.

Find potential customers by asking your friends and family members to tell others about your home-based baking/cooking business. You may also want to create a website and a blog. Fliers and newspaper advertisements are a good way to spread the word about your business.

Opening a home kitchen can be a complicated process. Each state has its own laws governing the opening of an in-home business and kitchen, and laws may vary from city to city. You will be required to have your commercial kitchen certified by your state's department of health in almost all locations.

Equipment

- Commercial kitchen with stoves, refrigerators, and utensils designed for your product
- Packaging Material
- Labels
- Phone
- Delivery Vehicle
- Concession Trailer or Truck (only for concessions)

The SBA (Small Business Association) may be able to help you with contacts for certification. Before considering kitchen certification, check on state, city and even neighborhood laws to find out if there are laws against operating a small business from your home.

Convert your kitchen into a commercial kitchen. Most requirements for commercial kitchens include regulations for sink size, counter space and floor space. Every state, city, and even county in the United States has variant regulations for the requirements of a commercial kitchen. To inquire about the regulations of your given area, contact your city or county planning department. Licensing information can also be found at each state's department of licensing websites. The licensing department in your state will also be able to provide you with information on food safety requirements including inspections, tax and insurance requirements, licensing and laws.

Once you have made the proper legal inquiries into your rights to open and maintain a home business in your area, you will need to have your commercial in-home kitchen inspected by your state's department of health. Inspections are often meticulous, however, once the guidelines are met, your kitchen will be up and running.

When preparing food, always err on the side of cleanliness and sanitation. Caution and good practice will pay off.

Income

There really is no "average" income for a home-based kitchen. Your income is dependent on what you make, where you sell it and the demand for what you are selling. To get a good estimate of what you may earn, write a business plan. The example below is for a concession stand but it can fit any product you might make.

If the food cost is 25%, energy (propane & electric) 5%, Insurance 2.5%, misc, paper, and condiments 2.5%. You sell 30 orders per day @12.00 = $360.00 for 240 days per year is $86,400.

- Food cost $21,600
- Energy $4,320
- Insurance $2,160
- Misc $2,160
- Expenses $30,240

    Your labor income is $56,160 if you have no debt.

Your business made a profit of $56,160, some of which should be put back into the business for upkeep and improvements. You may have considerably more profit if you have no debt. The debt should be paid quickly to increase your bottom line. There are many specialties in a home kitchen and you can calculate costs for your specific business by writing a business plan and including the expenses and estimated income for your business. You may want to start small and see what the demand is for your product.

People are willing to pay a premium price for many homemade items such as organic bread, cakes, cookies, jams, and many other goodies. Your prices should be higher than the grocery store prices for these items.

Massage Therapist

There are many reasons to become a massage therapist. It is a personally rewarding business to make people relaxed and happy, while at the same time earning a nice living. You will be helping people reduce the amount of stress they have in their lives. There are several different types of massage; these include neuromuscular massage, relaxation massage, sports massage and reflexology.

Skills

Most states, but not all, regulate massage therapy in the same way as other health care. This means you must be very careful to ensure that you meet the requirements. There are many courses which you can take to improve your massage techniques. Each state is different and you will need to comply with different requirements. Some states require 500 to 1000 hours of training and some require none.

Equipment

Once you have massage therapy training you can set up your own spa or massage center. Check zoning for your neighborhood to see if you can have a home business. Other than your training, a massage table, massage cream and decorations for your massage room is all that is needed. If the room is cool, you may want some light weight blankets and a small heater. You will need a number of sets of sheets and head rest covers since sheets will be changed and washed between each client. It is a good idea to wash with fragrance-free detergent called "Free & Clear" and to not use fabric softener which contains chemicals and artificial fragrances. These fragrances and chemicals can cause some severe allergic reactions to people who are sensitive to them and also cause problems with asthmatics. Many major laundry detergent makers offer free and clear detergent for the same price as those with fragrances.

Start by marketing your business in your neighborhood. You can offer some complimentary massages initially as well as offer family packages.

You can work in a formal medical environment if you prefer. Some massage therapists rent a room next to doctor's offices or physical therapist's offices. Massage therapists also work with psychologists, doctors and chiropractors to improve the health of a patient's back. You might want to work in physical therapy centers, rehabilitation centers, or even colleges.

Some massage therapists are mobile and visit the customer's home to perform the massage. This provides some much needed relief for many stressed people who may not be able to travel or do not have time to travel. It is even possible to set up in airports, malls and other locations as a way to offer quick massages to people who do not have time for a total massage. You will need a special chair for this type of massage. Hand out your cards so people getting quick chair massages know how to contact you for a longer massage.

Income

The salary range for a massage therapist is $20,000 to $102,000. Rates are by the hour or 45 minutes and range from $35 to $100. The rate you charge will be dependent on the area where you live and the amount of your experience and training. You must have an outgoing, pleasant personality that people enjoy being around. Many of your clients will be long term and come every two weeks to once a month.

Associations

American Massage Therapy Association (AMTA) -- http://www.amtamassage.org/index.html
Associated Bodywork and Massage Professionals (ABMP) -- http://www.abmp.com/home/
International Massage Association (IMA) -- http://imagroup.com/

Organic Dog Food & Treats

People think of their dogs as part of the family and want to feed them healthy foods. Feeding pets a healthy diet encourages good health and prevents visits to the veterinarian. Supplying these foods can mean big profits for a dog food business owner. Starting an organic dog food business is a great way to earn income and feel good that you are contributing to the health of pets.

Pet owners became much more aware in 2007 when pets died from eating food that contained imported wheat gluten and rice protein contaminated with melamine. The poisonous contaminant appeared in some brands sold as being natural. Since that time, the organic pet food business has been growing and many are becoming educated as to what is in their pet food. There are no regulations governing the word "natural" on pet food labels. Pet foods marketed as organic must meet the same U.S. Department of Agriculture standards as human food in the organic category, according to the USDA. Check on the regulations before you advertise your food as organic.

Skills

Find or create recipes that will be used for the dog food or treats. Test each recipe on your four legged friends. Consider how your recipes can be changed to develop several different flavorings and test again. The skills needed are fairly simple in finding your recipes, testing them, and then marketing. Decide how you want to sell as far as packaging and portions. The next step is marketing and you will need to decide whether to sell online, from your home, or in stores. Some successful dog food makers sell with overnight delivery on dry ice. Research which type of sale works best for you and what your product should cost. Include all costs in your pricing like ingredients, packaging, tags, and marketing. Organic dog food can even be found for sale on Amazon. Some fresh organic dog food is packaged on a tray similar to chicken and wrapped the same in plastic. Packages can be sold frozen and delivered with dry ice. Baked treats can be sold in plastic or paper bags.

Equipment

You will need the following equipment for your organic/natural dog food and treat business. The computer is listed mostly for marketing and research purposes, but it may not be necessary for everyone.

- Computer
- Printer
- Phone
- Fax
- Bone cookie cutter
- Baking pans
- Mixing bowls
- Recipe ingredients

- Mixing utensils
- Measuring utensils
- Packaging materials
- Tag materials
- Oven

Income

There are no published income statistics for this business. Calculate the estimated cost for each product. Keep a notebook with each recipe and all of the information including pricing and instructions. Testing your ideas will be inexpensive and if you have dogs, you will be testing your recipes on them. It is difficult to predict your income since there are different ideas on recipes, packaging, and marketing. People are willing to pay a premium price for organic dog food. Complete your price research before you decide where your price points should be.

NOTE: Please refer to my websites for business resources, books, courses, software, equipment and supplies for the businesses in this book.   From time to time additional business opportunities will be posted on my website. I hope this information makes the research for your new business easier. Clicking on the links in the websites will take you to resources for each item.

> http://www.pdsloss.com/
> http://www.RealisticHomeBusinesses.com/

Chapter 12

Home Workshop/Studio

Blacksmith/Welding Business

Starting a blacksmith business involves making different types of items made of iron, steel, wrought iron and cast iron. A welder can work with those materials and more, such as aluminum. A blacksmith typically uses more old-fashioned tools such as a forge and a welder uses electric or gas powered welders and cutters. You could make iron and steel items, repair metal items as well as create artwork made of metals.

The term blacksmith has also been used interchangeably with farrier. A farrier (horseshoer) provides horse shoeing services for horse owners. Farriers who use a forge to hot shoe (manipulate the shape of the shoe with heat) are considered blacksmiths. A farrier's profession is much different than the role of a traditional blacksmith who concentrates on metalwork.

Skills

Knowledge of blacksmithing or welding is needed along with experience in using the equipment. Having previous skills is imperative as this profession requires a lot of knowledge and practice.

Equipment

Proper tools and safety equipment are necessary to complete a project creatively and effectively. Tools are available for bending, cutting and joining different types of metal. Your project will dictate the tools needed. Here are some of the tools of the trade.

- Propane Forge
- Hammers
- Anvils
- Welders
- Plasma Cutters
- Safety Hoods
- Welding Gloves
- Metal Moving Equipment
- Assorted Small Tools

Income

The average income for a welder with an independent shop is $40 to $60 an hour.   It is harder to find an average income for a blacksmith or welding artist but your income will be tied to the quality of your art and how well you market your business.

Make a portfolio of your work for prospective customers. Market your business with professional business cards and flyers. After your business becomes established and you have several customers, word of mouth will bring more business.

If you make metal artwork, sell at art shows, farmer's markets, craft shows, and flea markets to market your business. Garden centers and nurseries are also a good outlet for metal art.

Associations

National Blacksmith and Welders Association --
http://www.arcat.com/arcatcos/cos40/arc40213.html
Artist Blacksmith Association of North America --
http://www.abana.org/

Candle Maker

Candle making is a lot of fun but also a lot of work. There are many
stores devoted to candles, holders, and accessories. The best
location is in a larger city near the most affluent neighborhoods. If
you are operating this business at home, you must be good at
marketing.

Skills

A successful candle maker must be creative, self-motivated, a
people person, and outgoing. Unless you have a business location,
it is necessary to find ways to market your candles. One of the best
marketing tools is a website with professional pictures of your
candles. You can also market at craft shows, fairs, flea markets, and
community events.   Market your candles in local art galleries,
boutiques, gift stores, hair salons, nail salons, and hospitals.
Another option is selling online with eBay, Etsy or Art Fire. A more
detailed description of how to set up shop online is in Chapter 14 of
this book. This is a good business to start part time and grow into
full time with repeat customers.

Equipment

The equipment needed to make candles requires a small
investment. Most of your supplies and equipment can be found
online. Here is a partial list of equipment.

- Beeswax

- Soy Wax
- Paraffin Wax
- Melting Pots
- Candle Moulds
- Candle Wick
- Candle Making Fragrance
- Candle Making Dye
- Candle Jars
- Packaging

Listed below are companies where you can purchase your candle making supplies.

Aztec International Candle Supplies -- http://www.candlemaking.com/store/Candlemaking/
Candles and Supplies -- http://www.candlesandsupplies.net/
Lone Star Candle Supplies -- http://www.lonestarcandlesupply.com/
Candlewic -- http://www.candlewic.com/
Wholesale Supplies Plus -- http://www.wholesalesuppliesplus.com/Candle-Making-Supplies.aspx

Income

A candle making business will average $5,000 to $10,000 a year but with excellent marketing, could bring in as much as $50,000 a year. Dedicated marketing and keeping on top of current trends is very important. Have a line of beeswax and soy candles for people who want all natural products.

Embroidery Business

If you enjoy sewing and embroidery, this business may be perfect for you. An embroidery business is simple to start, but there are steep upfront costs for equipment, training and inventory. You can create designs with software and transfer these designs using your embroidery machine to produce high quality embroidered products. Plan your business carefully to reach interested customers with your products. Statistics show over 70% of Americans wear embroidered or printed clothing everyday.

Skills

You do not need special skills to operate embroidery equipment or a digital printer, just proper training and experience. With the new embroidery machines and digital garment printers on the market, applying embroidery and logos is easy. Producing high-quality, commercial embroidery and digital prints takes time to master. You will need training on the equipment you purchase, some of which comes with the equipment. You may need more training depending on the sophistication and complexity of the machine and your current skill level. People may want names embroidered on hats, jackets, t-shirts, quilts, or any number of items. Gain experience on numerous items and thicknesses of fabrics before you offer your services to customers. You would not want to ruin an item belonging to a customer.

Equipment

The embroidery business has an upfront cost of $10,000 to $50,000 for equipment and inventory. Research well to be sure there is a large enough potential market and you can charge enough to make a profitable business in your area.

You will need an embroidery machine, which costs $8,000 to $14,000; design software that costs $600 to $15,000, averaging $3,500; small tools and equipment like needles and hoops, for $300 to $2,500; and an inventory of hats, T-shirts, uniforms or other types of items you might be embroidering. You will also need training on the equipment you purchase, some of which comes with the equipment. You may need to take additional training depending upon the sophistication of the machine and your current skill level. Visit your nearest commercial sewing machine business to view all of the machines available. They may even have a good used machine. Purchase a commercial machine and not a home machine.

Buying an embroidery machine is more complicated than it looks. Today's embroidery machines come with a host of different options for software. Packages range from basic embroidery to those that are capable of full color complex designs. Choose an embroidery machine that can grow with your business and has the ability to upgrade software as improvements come along.

Investigate your competition and determine if there is a gap in the market. There may be large embroidery factories serving a variety of customers. This might leave room for someone doing smaller custom projects for local schools or businesses. You might find small custom shops in your area but no one to take on large jobs for corporate clients. You can choose to focus on simple designs like monograms, or create beautiful and detailed art designs for upscale boutique dresses or bridal gowns. Team up with a local seamstress making tailor-made clothing that needs embroidery work for the final touches on her line. Local clubs sometimes sell jackets with their name and logo.

Check local zoning if customers will come to your home. Most embroidery orders can be picked up and delivered or sent but you may want a storefront. Word of mouth is one of your best advertising methods. You may want to start with a press release in your local newspaper. Other advertising methods are print ads, mailers, newspaper ads, television and radio and the Internet. A professional website is almost a requirement for any business. Include professional pictures of samples of your work on your website and on marketing materials.

Income

The income for an embroidery professional ranges from $18,000 to $57,000. The range is wide since your income is dependent on how well your business is marketed and the area where you live. If you live in a small town, the only way to increase your income is to offer services online. Contact organizations to see if they are interested in having their name and logo on jackets and hats, which you will ship individually to each customer.

Associations

Embroidery Trade Association -- http://embroiderytrade.org/
National Network of Embroidery Professionals --
http://www.nnep.net/

Gourd Artist

Becoming a gourd artist is one of the easiest types of craft business to start. You can turn gourds into works of art, bowls, birdhouses, candleholders, ornaments, lamps, dolls, and more.

Gourd art uses various mediums. It is possible to spray gourds with paint, or finish them with a variety of finishes including wax, varnish, or leather dye. They can be adorned with jewels, seeds, stones, or stitching.

Skills

You must be artistic to succeed in this business. Proficiency in the operation of small hand tools is also a must. Books are available that will stimulate your imagination.

Equipment

There are only a few tools needed for this business that make manipulating gourds easier. See the partial list below.

- Jig Saw
- Utility Knife
- Sander
- Carver
- Drill
- Wood Burning Pen
- Dust Mask
- Colors and Finishes
- Brushes and Applicators

Welburn Gourd Farm --
http://www.welburngourdfarm.com/toolsandsupplies.aspx
Sawdust Connection -- http://www.sawdustconnection.com/gourd-art-supplies.htm
Turtle Feathers -- http://turtlefeathers.net/

Income

There is no published average income for this business. Nice pieces sell from $50 to $500 each. This is a good business to make extra income. Your business growth will depend entirely on your artistic ability and marketing. If you can display your work in upscale shops in tourist towns or art galleries, you may do very well. A well designed website is another selling avenue. Find a way to set yourself apart from the competition. Extra income can also be made by teaching classes.

Jewelry Designer

People like handmade, one-of-a-kind jewelry. You could turn your jewelry making hobby a home-based business. Settle on your signature style or specialty -- create pieces with beaded design, hammered metal, stainless steel, silver or gold.

It is not hard to start a jewelry making business from home. The components, tools, and finished products are small and easy to store and transport. Most people can operate from one room in their home or even use the dining room table to begin their business.

Do not think of your products as "homemade," but rather handcrafted by an artisan. Handcrafted products are in demand, because they provide customers with a quality not often found in mass produced jewelry. Handcrafted jewelry sells for a premium since customers are willing to pay for something unique.

Skills

Your most important skill is using your creativity. Beads on a string are not going to be hot sellers. Pick a niche for your signature style and obtain the skills to make the pieces such as soldering, hammering, beading, using a rolling mill, or designing and firing metal clay. Some think jewelry is as easy as stringing beads on a wire but it is far from that easy. Buying all of the tools in the world will not make you successful unless you have the creativity it takes. The skill to select pleasing colors and shapes is important. Take some classes online, on DVD, or in person, if you are not already skilled in jewelry making. The second most important skill is marketing. Beautiful pieces sitting on your workbench have no way of being sold without good marketing.

There are a number of avenues for marketing your jewelry. Research craft fairs and booths, flea markets and community events. Market your jewelry by displaying in local art galleries, boutiques, hair salons, nail salons, and hospitals. Sell online with your own website, Etsy, or Art Fire. See Chapter 14 of this book for a more detailed description of how to set-up your shop in Etsy. Don't forget to wear your own jewelry everywhere you go; you are your best advertisement.

Equipment

Some types of jewelry making do not require many tools. Beading would be one niche that requires few tools where as metal clay requires specific tools and a kiln. Buy the appropriate tools and materials for your niche. Here are some of the more common tools, but keep in mind, you only need the tools that relate to your specialty.

- Pliers
- Hammers
- Torch
- Firebrick/Soldering Block
- Anvil
- Rawhide Mallet
- Kiln
- Flex Shaft Tool
- Pickle Pot
- Copper Tongs
- Tumbler
- Crimp Pliers
- Glue
- Thread
- Wire
- Rolling Mill
- Bead Loom
- Mandrels—Ring, Bracelet, or Neck
- Ring Sizer
- Marketing Materials—Displays, Gift Boxes/Packaging

Income

The average income of a jeweler is between $19,000 and $57,000. Pick your niche carefully and have some very unique pieces to sell. Market your items using high-quality photos and well designed cards and marketing materials. Combining online marketing with local marketing will provide the highest chance for success.

Associations

Jewelry Design Professionals' Network -- http://www.jdpn.org/
Women's Jewelry Association --
http://wjamarion.memberlodge.com/

Sewing Business

A sewing business is a great home based small business for anyone who is creative and loves sewing.   Specialize in one or two areas of sewing.   Here are some of the specialties you might want to consider.

- Alterations
- Altering/Making Drapes
- Bridal Fitting
- Hemming Trousers
- One Hour Sewing Lessons for Children & Adults
- Personalizing Clothing
- Quilts
- Tailor Made Clothing
- Custom Pillows

Create a price list for every service you offer; this will state exactly what services you offer and how much you charge. For services that are not on the list, calculate a price to compensate you for the number of hours it will take to complete the job.

Skills

Sewing skills and the knowledge of sewing machines and fabric types are needed for this business. Knowledge of which presser feet and attachments are appropriate for different fabric types and jobs is essential.

There are many items you can make if you do not want to do alterations.

- Baby Clothing
- Maternity Clothes
- Plus Sized Clothing
- Tall Sized Clothing
- Household accessories
- Bags or cases

Equipment

To start a sewing business, one or more machines are needed along with a table suitable for cutting out patterns or projects. If your business includes sewing or altering garments, a room with privacy is needed where people can try on clothes. A full-length mirror is necessary; if there is enough space, a three-way mirror would be better. If you give lessons, a place is needed where several people can sit in front of machines. Listed below is some of the equipment you may need.

- Sewing Machine
- Serger
- Cutting Mat
- Rotary Cutter
- Scissors
- Thread
- Dress Form
- Steam Iron
- Ironing Board

If you are working at home, an area is needed where strangers will be welcome. Keep pets out of this room. A pick up and delivery service to boutiques is nice to keep traffic to a minimum. Make sure you have the necessary insurance for your home business.

There are many different places you can market your business.

- Men's Clothing Stores
- Upscale Department Stores
- Western Stores
- Wedding Boutiques
- Interior Design Consultants
- Furniture Stores
- Boutique Clothing
- Craft shows

Once your business is established, consider areas for expansion. You could even offer one-hour sewing classes to children or adults if you wanted.

Income

The average income for a sewing business ranges from $20,000 to $60,000. Your income will depend on which specialty you choose, the quality of your work and the area where you live. Unless you are making items for sale, your market will probably all be local. If you are making items for sale, you can list them on a website like Etsy for handmade items. For more information on how to sell your handmade items on Etsy, refer to Chapter 14 in this book.

Associations

Association of Sewing and Design Professionals --
http://www.paccprofessionals.org/

Soap Making

Soap making is an easy business to start. Many people want to use natural products and are searching for natural old-fashioned soap. Natural soap does not dry the skin like commercial soaps since glycerin is left in the soap. Commercial soap makers extract the glycerin and sell it separately, which is what makes their soap drying to the skin. There is a good market for homemade soap and many places to sell your product.

Skills

There are only two ingredients required to make soap, fat and lye. In the past, soap was made once or twice a year. Originally, all soap was made from animal fats such as lard from pigs and tallow from cattle. Today oils are extracted from vegetables, grains and nuts providing an alternative to animal oils. Vegetable oil soaps are of a higher quality than soaps made with animal fats.

One of the best marketing tools is a website with professional pictures of your soap. You can market at craft shows, fairs, flea markets, and community events.   Market your soap in local art galleries, boutiques, gift stores, hair salons, nail salons, and hospitals. Another option is selling online with eBay, Etsy or Art Fire. See Chapter 14 for a detailed description of how to set up shop online. This is an excellent business to start part time and it will grow with repeat customers.

Equipment

Below is a list of equipment and supplies. This is an inexpensive business to start. You may not need all of these supplies depending on what type of soap you choose to make.

- Soap Moulds
- Oils & Butters

- Packaging & Labels
- Pans
- Gloves
- Thermometer
- Mask
- Melting pot
- Mixers
- Scale
- Soap Cutter

Listed below are some of the companies where you can purchase soap making supplies.

Aztec International Inc. -- http://www.candlemaking.com/store/Soap-Lotions-More-C3.aspx
Candles and Supplies -- http://www.candlesandsupplies.net/Soap-Making
Wholesale Supplies Plus -- http://www.wholesalesuppliesplus.com/Soap-Making-Supplies.aspx

Income

There are no average incomes listed for the soap business but if your marketing is good, you can expect a nice side income from this business. You can also specialize with the use of certain materials such as natural or organic. This specialty will make your products unique and exclusive. You will have clientele coming to you specifically for products, creating a recurring source of income. Packaging and presentation is also a large part of marketing soap. Start your business small and grow with repeat customers. People have turned their soap business into a large companies.

Quilt Business

Many people use quilts to keep warm. What could be better than to have a custom-made quilt in the winter when it is cold outside. Starting your own quilt business can be a great way of making some extra money. It might be difficult to make a living making quilts but the Internet has made it possible to reach customers anywhere. Quilt making is a very time consuming business and it may be hard to make a good income for the time you have to put into making them.

Sales Possibilities

- Friends & Family
- Wedding Gifts
- Birth Gifts
- Gift Shops
- Furniture Stores
- Antique Stores
- Craft Shows

Skills

The skills needed for quilting are sewing and quilting experience. Knowledge of your sewing machine and quilting machine are also important. You must have a good eye for colors since even the most beautifully sewn quilt will not look attractive if the colors clash.

Equipment

- Sewing Machine
- Quilting Machine
- Cutting Mat
- Rotary Cutters

- Scissors
- Patterns
- Quilt Rulers
- Quilting Designs
- Quilting Templates

Income

This would be a hard business to make substantial money. However, it is very satisfying to produce quilts that will be handed down for generations. Quilts are very time consuming to make but with the right market, it would be a nice extra income business.

You can also make other quilted items such as place mats, pot holders, wall hangings, bread baskets, covers, table runners, oven mitts, pillows, tote bags, diaper bags, jackets and vests. Enter contests and have plenty of business cards available to give to potential customers.

Painting/Art Lessons

Anyone who is good at painting can use their skills and turn it into a profitable painting lesson business. Painting lessons may not provide a living wage but is a nice way to make extra money. To earn more money, offer group painting lessons. If you are a "name" artist, you will be able to charge considerably more than an unknown artist.

Skills

You do not need formal training to offer painting lessons but you should be skilled at painting and teaching. Talented artists do not necessarily make good teachers. You do not need to be a well-known artist to offer lessons but you need to be skilled and confident to teach. Your personality should be outgoing and enthusiastic.

Equipment

The equipment needed for painting will depend on the type of painting you will be teaching. The equipment is listed below for several types of painting and you can select the supplies that fit your niche.

- Oil Paints
- Water Color Paints
- Acrylic Paints
- Canvas or Appropriate Paper
- Brushes
- Spatulas
- Cleaning Jars
- Paint Thinner
- Aprons
- Easel

Since painting supplies are expensive, it is preferable to have students furnish their own supplies but you will still need your own to demonstrate methodology.

Income

It is hard to predict or even list an average income for this business. Your income will be tied to your skills as a painter and teacher plus how well you market. You may choose to teach children or adults in your customer's home or your studio. There are many factors which will affect your income but there are many parents willing to spend huge sums on their children's hobbies. Another idea for income is to make a DVD or set of DVDs and sell them online.

Woodworking-Specialty Items

If you are talented at woodworking, making specialty items out of wood may be the business for you. There are different niches in the woodworking field which are all fairly easy to start.

Skills

You will need to know how to use the woodworking tools needed to make items in your niche. Having the right tool for each job will expedite your work and it will also look better.

Woodworking Niches

- Custom Spice Racks
- Custom Picture Frames
- Refinishing Furniture
- Show Cabinets for High End Guitars
- Specialty Cases and Cabinets
- Custom Furniture
- Wedding gift items
- Wooden photo albums
- Wooden Toys and Puzzles for Kids
- Small Scale Buildings for Railroad Buffs
- Bowls and Vases
- Clocks
- Wooden cases
- Jewelry boxes

There are many ways to market your products such as: craft shows, galleries, retail outlets, gift shops, or fairs. You may also choose to set a website where you can sell your creations online.

Equipment

The equipment needed for this business will depend on which niche you choose. You will need a workshop or garage since some of this equipment takes up a lot of space and you will have sawdust that should be contained. Listed are some of the more common tools.

- Table Saw
- Miter Saw
- Radial Arm Saw
- Router
- Drill Press
- Nail Gun
- Drill
- Hammers
- Sanders
- Planer
- Joiner
- Nail Sets
- Clamps
- Jigs
- Dust Collector
- Jig Saw
- Small Hand Tools
- Tape measures

Income

The income for a woodworker ranges from $15,000 to $39,500 a year. This is not a get-rich- quick profession but if it is something you are good at and enjoy, it might be perfect for you.

NOTE: Please refer to my websites for business resources, books, courses, software, equipment and supplies for the businesses in this book. From time to time additional business opportunities will be posted on my website. I hope this information makes the research for your new business easier. Clicking on the links in the websites will take you to resources for each item.

http://www.pdsloss.com/
http://www.RealisticHomeBusinesses.com/

Chapter 13

On An Acre or More

This chapter deals with professions that require land. Check your local zoning to verify agricultural or storage facilities do not violate zoning laws. The availability of water is also required for most of these businesses.

Egg Business

If you have always enjoyed the idea of farming, but did not want to invest in large, expensive farm equipment, an egg business might be the perfect solution. Organic eggs are very popular since people are trying to get away from the chemicals fed to commercial chickens. Being certified organic is complicated, where as calling your eggs natural from free-range chickens is simple. The organic tag means you must pass inspections and feed organic feed so make sure not to confuse "natural" with "organic." There is an excellent market for either natural free-range or organic labeled eggs.

Skills

Knowledge of chickens is necessary. If you have never been around chickens, be sure to get some good books and visit several poultry farms before you get into the business. You should have enough knowledge about chickens to know if the birds are sick and know what treatment should be given. If the chickens have something you are not familiar with, it is time to call a veterinarian. One house call from the veterinarian could quickly eat up your profit. Keep some portable cages in order to transport the chicken to the veterinarian instead of them coming to your ranch/farm. If you think a chicken is sick, isolate that chicken from the flock until it is well. Disinfect the area, feeder, water container, and bedding where the sick chicken was kept.

Be aware of the laws regarding egg selling in your municipality, county, and state. Call your county extension agent, state poultry, or agriculture specialist regarding local and federal laws. Inquire about the advertising claims and descriptions you make about your eggs and the conditions you must meet to make those claims. Sales permits may also be needed. In some locations, it is against the law to reuse other companies' egg cartons. You must go through a lot of inspections and expenses to use the "organic" label.

Equipment

This is a simple business to enter as far as equipment goes. Below is a list of things you will need. If you get larger, you will need more equipment and possibly an inspected handling room if you will be selling commercially to stores or the public.

- Chickens
- Coops
- Fencing
- Feeders
- Water Troughs
- Heat lamps
- Packaging-cartons

Determine how many hens you want in the beginning. Each hen will average two eggs every three days. To produce 700 eggs a week, 175 hens are needed. The hens will not lay that many eggs year round. Plan on around 180 eggs per hen per year.

Build a chicken house. If you have not had chickens before, there are good plans for chicken houses in books. No matter where you live, the chickens will need to have a house and provided with warmth. You will need two square feet for each hen. Start with a few chickens if you have not had them before. Starting with 100 chickens would be overwhelming and you would be inundated with unsold eggs if you had not developed your market. Include room for future growth and additional hens in your building plan. Check your zoning to make sure chickens are allowed in the quantities you want. Agricultural zoning is probably a requirement.

Enclose the land surrounding the hen house with chicken wire fencing. This will allow the hens to move freely inside and outside without being able to escape or for predators to get in and kill your chickens. When your building and yard is completed, purchase your initial chickens. Find a veterinarian who is competent on the care and illnesses of chickens to have someone to call if problems occur. Be aware that not all veterinarians are knowledgeable about chickens.

Income

In the beginning, your "egg money" may only be enough to pay for feed, supplements, miscellaneous expenses and free eggs for you and your family. When the word spreads to family and friends, you should start to see more money coming in than going out. At that time, think about increasing the number of chickens.

A dozen free-range eggs sell for an average of $3.50. Some locations get up to $6.00 a dozen for organic free-range eggs, while other locations are $3.00 a dozen. A 50 pound bag of organic chicken feed costs approximately $17. Check with your local feed store for prices in your location.   Six chickens will eat about a bag in about a month, which equals 8.3 pounds of feed a month per chicken. Selling six dozen eggs a month would pay for feed and miscellaneous supplies. Miscellaneous costs consist of egg cartons, bedding, water, power, supplements and supplies, which add relatively little to the monthly bill. Be very careful using the word "organic" unless your farm is certified. You can use the words "natural and free range" without any certification. Organic chicken feed is more expensive than non-organic feed.

Find your break-even number to help price your eggs and decide if this business is right for you in your specific location. Estimate all of your expenses for the entire year including feed, production, marketing, promotion, packaging, and delivery costs. Feed will probably be your greatest expense, but also include one-time costs like coop building or remodels or fencing. Add all of the expenses together. An estimate of eggs per hen is an average of 180 eggs per year.   Multiply 180 by the number of hens you have to get your total number of eggs and divide that result by 12 to get your estimated total number of dozens for the year. Divide the total expenses by the number of estimated dozens to get the minimum price you would have to charge to break even. Add your profit to the break-even point. If that number is too high, you may want to cut some of your costs. Your location may not be conducive to this business if the local price per dozen is too low.

Gardening

If you love gardening and have the talent for growing vegetables and herbs, this business can provide some extra income. Since gardening is seasonal, you will only receive income when your crop comes in. Income may be spread out over several months by making items such as jam, pumpkin butter, decorated gourds, etc.

Make sure your property zoning will allow a large garden. Normally a garden or nursery business is considered "agricultural" zoning. Equally important is the availability of water for irrigation. Every state is different on water well laws. Your well may be classified as "household", which in Colorado, means you can only use it inside of your house. You cannot even have an outside faucet. A "domestic" well allows you to water a set amount of acre-feet of water per year. Some wells are classified as "irrigation, commercial or agricultural" and you can water a larger amount of acre-feet. There are separate permits or laws relating to drawing water from a stream or lake. Be careful not to go over the limit on water used. It is difficult if not impossible to have the usage of an existing well changed to an irrigation well and new permits are hard to come by.

Skills

You will need a strong back and gardening skills. A large garden requires more maintenance, weeding and picking produce. Knowledge of the plants you are growing and the fertilizer needed is important.

Equipment

- Tiller
- Small Tractor
- Hand Tools
- Fencing

Income

The income for this business varies depending on your location and size of your garden. This business would provide supplemental income rather than generating enough for a living unless you are large enough to have a truck farm. Increase your income by holding workshops on specific gardening techniques. In addition to garden vegetables and herbs, consider pumpkins and gourds. Gourd artists look for dried gourds which you can sell locally and on eBay or with your own website. Consider selling produce at farmer's markets, a roadside stand, or if you have a large amount, talk to your local grocery store. Word of mouth is a great advertisement.

Greenhouse

If you have a green thumb, some space, a source of water, a strong back, and ambition, you may want to try your hand at operating a plant nursery. Consider an organic/natural nursery. Many people do not like the chemicals that are being used and will pay a premium price for organic. Do watch using the "organic" name unless you are certified organic. You can use the word "natural" and advertise no pesticides or herbicides though.

Check zoning restrictions to see if a greenhouse is allowed. Normally a greenhouse or nursery business is considered "agricultural" zoning. Equally important is the availability of water for irrigation. Every state is different on water well laws. Your well may be classified as "household", which in Colorado, means that you can only use it inside of your house and you cannot even have an outside faucet. A "domestic" well allows you to water a certain amount of acre-feet of water per year. Some wells are classified as "irrigation, commercial or agricultural" where you can water a larger amount of acre feet. There are separate permits or laws relating to drawing water from a stream or lake. Do not go over the limit on water used. It is difficult, if not impossible, to have the usage of an existing well changed to an irrigation well and new permits are hard to come by. If you have a domestic well (in Colorado) you are allowed to water one acre foot (check your permit) and have a garden so one medium size greenhouse would be allowed in place of a garden. The greenhouse will use less water than a garden. A commercial well is needed for multiple large greenhouses.

A greenhouse business also lends itself to raising trees and shrubs. Unsold trees and shrubs can be carried over for next year's sales. Be careful that the roots do not freeze over the winter. You can do this by what is called "heeling in" the pots. This means pushing dirt up around the pots, which mimics the plant being planted in the ground. Another method, which is much easier, is called the "pot-in-pot" technique. There are two pots, the liner pot is what you plant your tree or shrub in and the socket pot is buried with the top rim of the pot just above ground level. The lighter liner pots with plants in them are inserted into the socket pot. The liner pot is sized so that the rim catches on the socket pot rim, which keeps the containers from jamming together. This system insulates roots from winter and summer temperature fluctuations and conserves irrigation water. Pot in pot containers will not blow over like conventional containers on top of the ground. Plants can be moved easily and a lot of labor time is saved.

Skills

Knowledge of plants is needed to be able to grow each variety of plant. Start slowly and learn as you go. You should be able to select seeds and know how to grow the plants. If you are new to this business, try a limited number of varieties the first year.

Do research in your local area to see what is selling, the size of pots, varieties, and what items are priced the highest. You can wholesale to nurseries, retail or a combination of wholesale and retail.

Make sure you have done your research and that you will have buyers for what you are growing. Develop relationships with the businesses who will buy your products. The agreement to purchase your plants may be verbal or written but make sure you have a place to sell what you are growing before you spend the money on seeds, containers, etc. Do not grow a greenhouse full of beautiful flowers with nowhere to sell them. You can market to retail nurseries, landscapers, stores, or retail your plants on your property.

Study the plant species you select to grow. Plant seeds/cuttings at the appropriate time to ensure blooming or maturity will occur at the beginning of your targeted sale date. Plant stake tags will be needed for your specific plant. Put one tag in each pot. These stakes have a picture of the plant in bloom, tell the buyer the plant name, and care instructions. Nurseries will not buy your plants without these professionally printed stakes. Stagger planting and transplanting if you want some plants to mature later in the season. Your main workload will start after January. The season slows greatly in July or August. There will be several months in the fall and winter with limited or no work.

Equipment

The first thing you will have to do is to construct a greenhouse. Find wholesale nursery suppliers in your area. Get to know your wholesaler since you will be, not only, buying a greenhouse but flats, pots, and a multitude of supplies. They are happy to send a sales person to meet with you. The sales person will evaluate your location and help with building ideas. They will deliver the greenhouse package and flats, pots, potting mix, etc. If you are near any nurseries, they will deliver most of your orders using their truck. Deliveries near larger towns are on a weekly or bimonthly delivery schedule. There are usually one to three wholesale suppliers in the larger cities of each state. You can search the yellow pages online to find them. It is not profitable to pay retail for your pots and supplies.

You can hire the supplier or their recommended construction people to build the greenhouse but it will be less expensive if you purchase the greenhouse materials, fans, heaters, louvers, etc. and then build it yourself or hire someone locally. You need to understand exactly how the greenhouse is built and how it operates, even if you do not build it yourself. Watch every phase of the greenhouse construction since you must rely on yourself if something breaks. You do not want to lose your whole crop if the inflation motor stops and the wind comes up. You should be able to change the motor yourself and you should have a spare on hand.

- Land for a Greenhouse
- Greenhouse
- Water Supply
- Plant Starting Equipment
- Containers
- Plant Tags
- Watering Equipment or System
- Delivery Truck/Trailer
- Tractor with Bucket
- Stakes
- Plant Tie Ribbon and Machine
- Backup Generator

Income

The greenhouse business is very lucrative. The wholesale income from a 24 by 26 foot greenhouse is limited to approximately $8,500 a year. With multiple larger hoop houses, your income can be over $250,000.

Note: I personally operated my own greenhouse for 5 years. I started with a small lean-to greenhouse attached to my barn that I built myself. The next year I had a greenhouse package delivered and built the greenhouse myself. Neighbors came over to help put the double layer of plastic on the outside and I had help lifting the heater. I have much more building experience than most women, but you can build a greenhouse yourself with a little help. I started with no experience and learned as I went. The more knowledge I gained, the more income I made. I also worked with some very nice retail nurseries, one of which helped me gain a lot of knowledge.

My first year in business I started with a small lean-to greenhouse attached to my barn. Mistake number one was I had no clue where I was going to sell the plants. I repotted huge beautiful Shasta Daises twice and later sat in a parking lot trying to sell them at the end of the season. I sold a few but still had a trailer load of them. I finally found a nursery willing to buy them but for a low price. The second season I made sure I knew what people wanted and had several nurseries lined up to buy my next year's crop. Later research showed that for my location, perennial flowers in flats brought the best price and second was tomatoes and peppers in number 1 pots. The last three years I was in operation I added small trees and lilacs in #2 pots and increased my income. The next step would have been another larger greenhouse had I not sold the property. I loved this business and think it is a good choice for anyone who loves growing plants.

Associations

Greenhouse Grower (trade magazine) -- http://www.greenhousegrower.com/
Greenhouse Associations are Regional – check for your state or region online

Horses Boarding/Training

Many part-time horse people dream of turning their love of horses into a profitable business. There are a number of opportunities related to the horse business from boarding facilities, horse training, feed stores, farriers (horseshoers), and saddle/tack shops. Each type of business requires its own set of skills. If you are considering this type of business, you will likely already have the needed skills.

This very labor-intensive business is a 24 hour a day, 7 day a week job. You need to love the lifestyle and like people to operate this business. Your insurance may be high and you will need bathrooms and possibly handicap access in most states.

Skills

If you are going to board or train horses, a good working knowledge of horses is definitely needed. It takes years of experience to become a horse trainer. If you have experience as a competitor, you could take a few horses in for training. People are always looking for a good trainer. Some do not have time to spend working with their horses and others do not have the knowledge or experience. Do not consider this business unless you are an accomplished horse person.

Horse boarding requires skills in horse health and horses in general. Your boarding facilities need to be well kept and safe to be appealing to someone looking for a place they trust to board their horse. Knowing their horse is in the care of an experienced horse person is important to the owners. Training and boarding businesses sometimes go hand in hand as a good business opportunity. Require your boarders to sign a liability waiver and boarding contract. Written recourse is needed if someone does not pay or if you are sued. All of their information should be on the boarding contract along with feeding instructions and their veterinarian information.

Selling feed and tack is an additional business. If you are a horseshoer, you can also shoe customer's horses if they like your work and not have to leave home. Design a business card and flyer describing your services to promote your business.

Equipment

- Horse Facility with Pastures and Stalls
- Home on the Property
- Arena
- Round Pen
- Small Tractor
- Hay Storage

- Frost Free Water Tanks & Faucets
- Cleaning Tools
- Room for Selling Tack Items
- Room for Selling Feed

Income

It is difficult to come up with an average income since there are so many variables. The prices in your local area may be entirely different from in another state.   Some trainers make large incomes and others much less.

Horse boarding costs between $400 and $1,000 per horse per month with full care. Hay, grain bedding, watering, turnout, and stall cleaning are included in full care boarding. The barns, stalls, fencing, round pens, and arenas are expensive to build and maintain. If you can add training services or rent your arena for competitions and shows, the additional income will help your bottom line. Check the going rates in your local area that have the same extras that you provide, such as an arena, round pen, and riding space, to get a basis for estimating what your income would be for the amount of stalls or pens you have. Remember to save several pens back if you are training for incoming horses. Facilities are the largest expense, with feed costs second.

Natural Beef

Organic and natural beef is one of the fastest-growing sectors of the natural foods market. Organic beef is defined as beef that is fed only certified organic grasses and grains, have outdoor access, and are free of hormones and other drugs used in mainstream cattle production. The term "natural" means absolutely nothing. Advertise natural and list how the animal is fed, no hormones or drugs are used, and if the beef only fed on pasture or was also fed grain. Making money raising organic beef is an endeavor for someone interested in helping to create alternatives to the unhealthy and somewhat questionable mainstream meat industry. This business is usually operated on a smaller scale than industrial processors but a higher price is received for your cattle. Be careful labeling or advertising your beef as "organic" if it actually just "natural". To use the word organic, you must be certified "organic" which is a lengthy expensive process. You may want to start by calling your beef natural and describing what and how it is fed or that hormones and drugs are not used. During this time, you can start the organic certification.

Contact your state Department of Agriculture regarding fees and requirements for certification as an organic beef producer. Your local USDA office can assist in finding an organic certifier in your area. They will inspect your property and feeding plan to assure you are feeding and raising strictly organic beef. If your property passes inspection, your operation will be certified as an organic beef producer, and you will be allowed to sell your organic beef on the general market.

Skills

Most people starting in this business are already ranchers/farmers and have livestock knowledge. Keep records on each animal for organic certification purposes. Verification on where each animal originated is needed. Keep all of your invoices from organically grown feed. Records must demonstrate that your animals received no antibiotic treatments. Occasionally you will have to treat a sick animal. They can be sold along with commercial cattle who probably received much more than one treatment of antibiotics. Have a corral for isolation purposes in case you do get a sick animal.

Start a website advertising your beef whether it is natural or certified organic. Market your beef with flyers and business cards. Word of mouth will be your best advertisement. Make sure to comply with all of the regulations of your State and the USDA when selling meat.

Equipment

This is a partial list of what you will need to raise organic/natural beef. You may also use a horse or a four-wheeler to move your cattle. You will likely raise your own calves since you will know your own animal's treatments.

- Pasture Land
- Cattle
- Corrals
- Barn
- Hay Storage
- Tractor
- Scales (if you want to weigh before shipping)
- Fencing
- Squeeze Chute

Income

The average income of a rancher is $50,000. Income is dependent on the land you own or rent, buildings, fences, and corrals needed, and how many head of cattle you own. You may need to purchase a tractor to bring feed to your cattle and a squeeze chute to ear tag and brand. You can expect a higher income for organic/natural beef than a regular rancher. There are many variables in ranching that affect income.

Associations

Organic Trade Association --
http://www.ota.com/organic/foodsafety/OrganicBeef.html

Agricultural Marketing Resource Center --
http://www.agmrc.org/commodities__products/livestock/beef/org
anic_beef.cfm
National Cattleman's Association -- http://www.beef.org/
National Cattleman's Beef Association --
http://www.organicguide.com/organic/tag/national-cattlemens-
beef-association/

Pet Sitting/Training

If you love animals and want to start a related business, then
starting a pet sitting and/or pet training business might be the
perfect business for you.   Pet sitters take care of animals for either
the day or longer periods. Some people hire pet sitters every day
while they are at work and others only while they are out of town
on business or vacation.   Your responsibilities may include walking,
feeding, grooming and administering medications. You can offer
your services on your property or go to your customer's home. You
may want to take care of people's pets in their own home and not
on your property. That type of service does carry a lot of
responsibility since you will have the keys to someone's home. You
need to be bonded and insured. The bond will cover theft if you
employ anyone. Insurance will cover the client's pet and property.

Many people enlist the services of a professional dog trainer to help
train their dog. Professional dog training can help turn an unruly pet
into a well-behaved member of the family.

Skills

You will need animal handling skills along with animal health
knowledge. Knowing when an animal is not feeling well is
important since you are responsible for this animal's welfare while
the owner is gone. Before you take on the task of sitting for a large
dog, make sure you can handle the dog and that the dog is
comfortable with you. Many people will have more than one pet

under your care such as dogs, cats, and fish. Get specific written instructions from the owner on the feeding and care for each pet. Require the owner to furnish the name and phone number of their veterinarian and a number where they may be reached in case of an emergency. Be honest with clients requesting care for a species of pet you have never cared for. Have a list of what pets you will sit. Decide if you are comfortable working with all breeds of dogs and if you will take care of horses, birds, ferrets, snakes, fish, rabbits and other animals.

Understand people are making decisions, not only about letting a stranger into their home, but to care for their precious pet. They want to feel that you have the qualifications to take care of their pet and are trustworthy in their home.   Have all your pet sitting agreement forms and policies with you, but let your love and knowledge of animals show.

 If you are training pets, experience is essential. You may have a particular niche of training that you are experienced in such as showing, agility, puppy training, hunting dogs, or obedience training. There are a number of different types of training you can offer if you have the experience. A good track record of winning shows will make you popular and help you command a higher income.

Equipment

Equipment needs depend on if you are caring for someone's pet(s) at their home, your facility, or if you are training dogs. The following list is an example of equipment you may need. If you are training or showing dogs, you might consider making extra income by selling some quality or custom equipment. Make sure pets have all vaccinations.

- Vehicle capable of transporting pets
- Selection of collars and leads

- Kennel crates
- Emergency veterinarian supplies
- Niche equipment
- Kennel facility if boarding
- Accessories for facility (beds, bowls, supplies)

Make professional business cards and flyers describing all of the services you offer. Place an ad in your local newspapers, post cards in pet stores, dog grooming sites, local stores, restaurants, churches, and community buildings. Word of mouth will be one of your best advertisements.

Income

Pet sitters make $25,000 to $32,000 a year and dog trainers make from $27,000 to $52,000 a year. Your income is tied to your location. Check out your competition to see what rates are in your area. Here are some sample prices.

In home pet sitting
- $20 per visit (2 pets)
- $30 per day (2 visits)
- $5 each additional pet
- $10 per day additional for holidays—list them
- Some areas subject to mileage fee
- $10 Potty Breaks ($3 extra for additional pets)

Dog walking
- $14 for 30 minutes
- $12 for 30 minutes (weekly)
- $3 for each additional dog

Dog Training
- $75 per hour
- $150 for a set of classes

Below is a list of other services you may want to offer.

- Boarding at your facility
- Pet taxi
- Pooper scooper
- Grooming
- Puppy training
- Agility dog training
- Hunting dog training
- Obedience training
- People training

Associations

National Association of Professional Pet Sitters --
http://petsitters.org/
Association of Pet Dog Trainers -- http://www.apdt.com/
International Association of Canine Professionals --
http://canineprofessionals.com/

Pigeon Control

Catching pigeons can be a lucrative business. Pigeons are a common bird pest and cause a lot of damage.   Pigeon droppings deface and accelerate the deterioration of buildings, statues, monuments, and roofs, which increases the cost of maintenance. Pigeons located around airports can also be a threat to human safety due to potential bird and aircraft collisions. Large amounts of droppings produce a foul odor and may kill plants and grass. Pigeon manure on park benches, statues, monuments, fountains, cars, and unwary pedestrians is not only aesthetically offensive, but can cause health issues.   Pigeons consume and contaminate large quantities of food intended for human or livestock consumption near grain handling facilities and can carry and spread diseases to people and livestock through their droppings. The manure can also possess airborne spores that infect humans with a systemic fungal disease. They carry or transmit encephalitis, Newcastle disease, toxoplasmosis, salmonella food poisoning, and several other diseases. Pigeons carry parasites including various species of fleas, lice, mites, ticks, and other biting insects, some of which bite people.

A friend of mine had a business years ago controlling pigeons. You can easily make over $1,000 net profit a week contracting with apartments, businesses and building owners. Look for large buildings with flat roofs and pigeons nearby. Create a contract to use with the building owners.

The common pigeon was introduced into the United States as a domesticated bird, but many escaped and formed feral populations. The pigeon is now the most common bird pest associated with people. Federal law does not protect feral pigeons and most states do not protect them. Consult state and local laws before using any control measures. Some cities provide protection to all species of birds.

Pigeons are dependent on people to provide them with food and places to roost, loaf, and nest. They live around large apartment and office buildings, parks, city buildings, bridges, farmyards, grain elevators, feed yards and feed mills. They primarily eat grain and seeds but also eat garbage, livestock manure, insects or other food provided for them by people. They require about one ounce of water daily. They can consume their required daily intake of water from a condenser on the roof of a building but also frequent fountains, lakes, snow or standing water.

Skills

You will need very few skills for this business. Marketing is your most important ability. You will need to be able to convince the owners or managers of buildings that you can control their pigeon problem. Have a contract for your services. After your customer signs your contract, you will deliver cages, scatter feed, and put water container in the cage and leave. Check your cages every few days, take the birds out of your large cage, and put them in a smaller transport hard side cage to take home. Your cages will be located on rooftops where the pigeons are nesting.

Equipment

There is not a lot of equipment needed for pigeon control. A computer and office equipment is listed only so you can have a website, write contracts and keep track of your business but it is not required.

- Vehicle capable of holding large cages
- Cages
- Computer
- Printer
- Phone

You can build or buy traps. Homemade traps can be made of chicken wire with a plywood bottom and framed with 2x2's. Locate a trap door on top so you can get the birds out and cut holes on the sides. Form a funnel out of chicken wire to put on the sides. The birds will walk in the large end of the funnel and then cannot figure out how to get out. Locate the traps on the flat rooftops.

Use chicken scratch (commercial chicken feed) and pour on top of the trap after you set it in place on the roof. The birds will be able to eat a little of the food that spills out of the cage when you pour it in. They will have to walk in the funnel to the inside of the cage to get more. You must also have water available to the birds in the cage. Check the cages every 2 days. Collect the trapped birds and transfer them to another cage for removal. Put more feed out if necessary and make sure your container is full of water. If you have to walk through crowds of people, put the birds in an opaque solid cage to avoid any confrontations or problems with animal rights activists. Build large walk-in wire cages at your house to hold them.

You can catch them again with a fishing net. Now...what do you do with these birds? My friend sold them for $1 apiece to people training hunting dogs. They would teach their dogs to point with the pigeons.

Some people eat pigeons. They are especially popular with the French and Asian community. Pigeon that you eat is called squab. Squab is young pigeon with rich dark meat that is ideal for roasting or grilling. The recent price online is about $11.00 each when you buy 24 birds, They ship overnight. That price, in itself, is reason to consider raising pigeons. Many years ago, my grandfather raised pigeons and sold thousands of squab to local people.

As a last resort, humanely dispose of them using carbon monoxide or a carbon dioxide gas chamber. Poisoning with bait is regulated. Make sure you can obtain and use whatever poison you are considering. Most of this type of poison requires a license. Be sure to check with your state and local laws to make sure trapping and your method of disposal is legal. Poisoning birds is a complex task that requires a great deal of care. It should only be performed by someone who has the necessary training.

You may turn a lucrative pigeon capture business into a second equally lucrative business of raising squab. Some of the older birds may be sold for dog training.

Income

Your income will be tied to your location. This business will not work well in a small town but in a large city, you could make $60,000 a year. Research this business well before starting, but it has very low start up costs. If you can build your own cages from scrap wood and chicken wire and have a truck or van, you can be in business for under $100. You can hire people to pick up the captured birds and put out more feed.

Real Estate Clear-Out/Clean Up Company

Today's ailing real estate market is a good match for this business. Even in good times for the real estate market, this business will prosper. I have friends who work for themselves in this business and are overwhelmed with work. Today, there are many foreclosures, and many people leave their belongings in the house. Some are angry they are losing the house and leave a mess. There are usually many belongings and much junk to get rid of in order to prepare the house for sale. The mortgage holders need to find a reputable company or persons to do this work. Some renters leave a lot of furniture and junk behind. These properties cannot be rented again until the mess is cleaned up. A third use for this service is when someone dies. Sometimes the family comes and removes some items, but are overwhelmed. They often hire someone to complete the job.

Skills

The majority of this work comes from banks, mortgage companies, real estate companies, rental agencies, individual rental unit holders, real estate management companies, and families of deceased. You are expected to look at the house or property and bid on the cleanup and inclusions. It may only consist of hauling away a lot of excess stuff or may include cleaning down to the carpet and appliances. You will probably need to be bonded. A company name registered with the state you live in, cards, contracts and truck will be needed in order to look legitimate. You can do the haul away part of the job and hire someone to clean the house and possibly run a yard sale.

Equipment

You will need a truck and probably a trailer. A strong back is a plus or you will have to hire help. This business is a good match for a husband/wife team or family but can be done alone with a little hired help. While many items may need to be hauled to the dump, a number of treasures may be found during the process. Hired help must be trustworthy. Keep in mind some people hide cash and bonds in books and magazines. Have a large garage or storage unit for the better items that are worth keeping or selling. There are auctions where you can turn items into cash.

If you do not want to haul trash, you can hire a disposal company to furnish a large dumpster, which they will deliver and pick up when you call. A truck and trailer will still be needed to haul the items that can be salvaged.

Income

There is more than one way to make money from this service. First is the income from your bid for cleanup but an added benefit is that some of the "junk" they want you to haul off, may be worth something. A friend who actually has a business performing this service has had yard sales right on the property during cleanup. Since there were good yard sale items, he piled those items in the yard and hired someone to run the yard sale. He made $3,500 on his bid to clean up the property and house and $2,500 on the yard sale! That did not include some of the other better quality items sold elsewhere. That is a nice profit on one property.

Income could also be derived from checking the properties on a regular basis to insure there has been no vandalism and upkeep such as mowing weeds or lawns. These services can be another lucrative source of income.

NOTE: Please refer to my websites for business resources, books, courses, software, equipment and supplies for the businesses in this book. From time to time additional business opportunities will be posted on my website. I hope this information makes the research for your new business easier. Clicking on the links in the websites will take you to resources for each item.

http://www.pdsloss.com/
http://www.RealisticHomeBusinesses.com/

Chapter 14

Selling And Reselling

Antique Mall—Gift Mall Space

You can have your own retail shop at a fraction of the cost of renting a building. Mall space type stores have been introduced in the last 10 years. They are very popular because there is no liability like there is when renting an entire store. A large building is divided into many small sections that are rented by the square foot. Your landlord pays rent or owns the building, pays the utilities, insurance, and many times furnishes the help. The rent on your space is determined by the square footage in your space and usually the location in the building. Spaces towards the front are normally higher than in the rear of the building. Rents run from $75 to $200 a month, which includes utilities and normally someone is there to sell your items. Some malls require that you work one day a week and all of the people who rent spaces put in a day or so a week working in the store. Other malls use their own help. Be sure to have a good understanding of what is required before signing a rental or lease agreement. With a good location and the right inventory, you can expect to make $200 to $4000 or more per month. The most important idea of renting a space is the building LOCATION. Your business will sink or swim depending on your choice of location.

Skills

Marketing and location are the largest factors in making a successful business. You may have the nicest most popular merchandise and still fail if you are in a bad location.

What would you sell? Some people buy inventory to sell while others go to estate sales, auctions, moving sales and buy from classified ads. Many people sell what they make such as woodworking, photography, crafts, or gourd art. Craig's List is another place to look for nice inventory. Some people sell items that were handed down from a relative and they have no idea of what the item is worth. If you sell antiques, do some research to learn what to buy and where to price your inventory. There are many excellent books on antiques. Your shop may contain antiques or sell items with the same theme such as southwest, western, collectables, pottery, etc.

I know a number of people who have successful mall shops. I personally rented a space and was not as successful as friends who rented elsewhere, mainly because I did not know the pitfalls to look for. The key is, location, location, location.

The friends who were successful, most importantly, picked a location with a lot of traffic that were looking for their type of goods. The trick is to get the right kind of traffic for the items you are selling. A good location is an area where tourists gather. Small tourist towns get a lot of foot traffic. If you are in a larger city, select a location with upscale traffic and a good reputation. The people I know who are successful are selling small antiques, antique furniture, rustic furniture, antique dolls, memorabilia, art, handmade items, unusual jewelry, and niche crafted items. I have also seen hand-knit items, like hats and vests sell well in tourist town malls. Some regular retailers will let you sell your items in a small portion of the store or on a rack. Smaller items can sometimes be consigned and no rental of space is required. Several acquaintances rent space in a nearby town that tourists frequent. An excellent location is on main street during tourist season in a tourist town. You may want to rent in a small town nearby, but not necessarily, where you live. I know one person who makes a very good living renting space in three different stores in a tourist town.

My personal experience was only breaking even. The mall business was booming when I opened my store. The only space available was in a downtown location of a large city. The store had been recently remodeled and looked very nice when I went to look. There was a waiting list for the antique mall in a better location in town. In my eagerness to get started, I rented in the new mall. I set up, stocked, and decorated my little store. I was selling photography, jewelry, and southwest gift items. There were many compliments but not near the sales expected. I went to restock, straighten, and check inventory once or twice a week. While doing my weekly visits to check inventory, I began getting uncomfortable as I noticed what appeared to be homeless people loitering in the store to get warm.

At the end of two months, many people who had checked my booth told me that my inventory was far too nice for that particular store. I realized in my excitement to open a store that I had selected the wrong store in the wrong location. Renters started leaving since no one was selling nicer items. I cut my losses and closed my store. Other commitments stopped me from getting on the waiting list for the better malls.

If you do not work in the store, you should go in once or twice a week to check your inventory. Shoppers do not understand that the spaces belong to different people. They pick up an item wanting to purchase it, but after walking around, change their mind and put your item down in someone else's store. You will have to retrieve some of your inventory in other locations in the store. Always mark or tag your items well with tags that cannot be easily removed or replaced and if possible, a different color or size than others tags so they will be easy to spot.

Before signing a lease or contract, make sure you understand the requirements and conditions. Do you have to commit to a long-term lease? Find out if you are required to work in the store and make sure the schedule will work for you. Does the space come with a backdrop or will you have to section off your own space? You can make your divider out of lattice hooked together with large hinges from a local building supply but it is time consuming. The hinges will allow some adjustment of your panels and make your divider wall more stable. The lattice is more attractive and keeps people focused in your space when you staple lightweight material on the backside. Spray paint works wonders if you want a colored background. Check with the landlord to see what is allowed and if there is a height limitation. Keep your colors neutral so the focus is on your inventory, not the display. Your display will have a definite effect on perception of the quality of your inventory and draw people in or repel possible customers. While you do not want to spend a fortune on displays, be sure they make your inventory show well. Spend time in the store on different days of the week and talk to other renters. Make sure these renters are not also owners or you may not get a truthful answer. Most are happy to share experiences with you.

Equipment

The only equipment you need for this business are displays and backdrops. Normally you can build a wall with hinges tying the sections together out of lattice. You can make a very nice display without spending a lot of money.

Income

This is one business that your income will definitely be determined by your location and the popularity of the items you have for sale. There is no real average income but the people I know made from

$400 to $2,000 a month per store. Several of them had multiple locations, some in larger cities near nicer areas of town and others in smaller tourist towns.

Auctions

Auctions are a great way to find merchandise to resell for a profit. Even small towns have frequent auctions. Auction houses get a variety of goods from places such as estates, storage facilities, business closings, and people cleaning out their excess stuff. There are some real treasures. You will have to do research to know what things are worth.

Skills

Buying at auctions requires research to know the value of items. Avoid paying too much and ending up with a building full of unsalable stuff.

Locate the auctions in your area and go to several to see what kinds of items they have. Local auctions are normally listed in the classified section of your local paper. If your town is large enough, there may be a local auction house that has an auction once a week. Some auctions specialize in government surplus, business closures, antiques, estates, or farm and ranch. Estate auctions generally have the nicest quality of items but there have been some real treasures found at farm and ranch auctions.

Arrive at the auction site an hour early. Look around to inspect the items for sale and get your buyers number. Note the location of the items you are interested in buying to know when to start watching. There will be a desk or small building where you register for your buyer's number. They usually ask for your driver's license, address and phone number. You will be given a card with a number. When you bid and win an item, you will be asked for your number. At the end of the auction, the secretaries will have a list of your purchases and you will pay for those items. Do not forget to tell them it is for resale so there will be no tax charged. Furnish a copy of your tax license, when you sign up for your buyer's number. If you become a regular at their auction, you may be given a permanent number and will not have to sign in at each auction.

Be careful not to catch auction fever. It is easy to be caught up in the excitement when bidding and you can end up paying too much. Let the item go if the price gets too high. You are in business to make money on the item, not win the bid.

You can sell your purchases in a number of places such as Craig's List, local newspaper, eBay, Etsy (if it is an antique), your own garage sale, to a private party or business.

Equipment

There is not a lot of equipment needed for this business other than a truck and possibly a trailer for hauling your items. You will need a building or garage to store your purchases until they can be sold.

- Local Newspaper
- Computer
- Internet Connection
- Digital Camera
- Truck
- Trailer
- Garage or Storage Building
- Dolly & Cart

Some auctions only take cash, some checks, and others will accept credit cards. You are usually charged an extra premium for using a credit card, which may be 3%.

Income

Your income will be directly tied to how good you are at estimating the value of items you win.   It is hard to set an average income but if you are a shrewd buyer, you could make from $40,000 to $125,000 a year. Your income will also depend on your local market for buying and selling.

eBay

EBay is an online auction market. Many people make their living selling on eBay. There are opportunities for small businesses, entrepreneurs, and people just wanting to clean out their attics and basements. Many times what people would think to be old junk, sells for a premium price. It has become hard to sell new inventory and make much money on eBay. There is a lot of competition, which brings the price down. People who drop their price too low will be gone soon since it is a lot of work taking pictures, listing, selling, packaging, and shipping. You are not in the right niche or pricing correctly if you are not making much after the eBay and PayPal fees. Be sure to take eBay and PayPal fees into account when listing an item. Your asking price should be more than twice what you paid unless it is a more expensive item or the fees will eat into your profits.

Skills

Selling on eBay requires computer skills. You will need to write a description of the items you are selling. You must own and know how to operate a digital camera. Understanding how to take good pictures, uploading the pictures to your computer and possibly editing the pictures is important. After the picture is on your computer, you will need to add it to your listing. If the item you are selling is expensive, you should take pictures from different angles, sides and possibly the bottom and top. An example of an item that should have several of pictures would be an antique. If you have an item with an imperfection or crack, be sure to take a picture and explain the location.

After the pictures are taken, package the item for shipping and weigh the package. Free shipping can be included, but be careful in selecting the locations that you will ship free or you could make less on the item than your cost. Some items can be shipped in bubble pack envelopes while others will need a box. The post office will furnish free boxes if you are shipping priority mail. Use priority flat rate for shipping items that will fit in the box. The post office furnishes free priority envelopes, padded envelopes and small, medium and large boxes. When using regular parcel post, you can buy padded envelopes in bulk from eBay reasonably or pick up boxes from your local stores that they are discarding. Get sturdy boxes without much writing. Liquor boxes are not good to use since there are restrictions in sending liquids and liquor even if that is not what is in your box. Use a black marker to mark out any confusing text on used boxes.

You can sell your item for a set price or enter in an auction. You will have the choice of how many days your item will be available, which is the duration of the auction. The most widely used time frame is 7 days. That gives people enough time to look without having the auction time frame be too long. If you list for too long, it is possible for interested individuals to forget about your auction and miss the deadline.

Equipment

The equipment needed to sell on eBay is minimal and you will probably already have most everything but the scale.

- Digital Camera
- Computer
- Printer
- Bank Account

- Credit Card
- Scale to weigh packages

Sign up for an eBay account. Make sure to use a user id that will be descriptive, professional and fits your particular product. EBay offers training which you should take advantage of since it will save a lot of time. There are forums where you can ask questions. Even though learning the ropes can be frustrating, be courteous since people do remember what others have said. EBay owns PayPal but they are still separate businesses and you will have to set up separate accounts. I have fees charged to a credit card to avoid keeping track of fees in my bank account. If anything bad should happen, you can always dispute a credit card charge.

It is necessary to have a PayPal account to receive money or send money for items you purchase on eBay. I was hesitant to give out my bank and credit card information when I signed up but in 12 years, I have not had any problems. I did not want to give PayPal my regular checking account number so I started a new savings account and used that number. When a certain amount of money accumulates in savings, I transfer it to a checking account. If the very worst happens, no one can get into my regular accounts. In order to set this up, use the routing number of your bank, which is on the bottom left side of your checks. Instead of giving your checking account number, use the new savings account number. Furnish a credit card as a backup to your bank account with no worries since credit cards are protected. PayPal now requires a social security or EIN number if you make over $20,000 and sell 200 items. Using an EIN is a simple way to protect your social security number. Getting an EIN, described in Chapter 15 is simple and instant. If you furnish that information, they will send a 1099 to you and the IRS at tax time. Keep good records of purchases and the selling price. This is a business and any merchant account will require your personal information. If you sign up for their debit card, you will have to give your social security number, just like you would have to do with a credit card company or the bank. You are allowed to have two PayPal accounts. Having two accounts might be nice to keep personal and business sales separate but the 1099 eBay sends to the IRS will combine your income.

To become familiar with eBay, sell several of your attic or basement items. Then buy a few small items. It is good to have feedback as a buyer and seller before trying to sell any important merchandise. Good feedback is important, since people decide if they want to buy from you by looking at your track record. Be very truthful when listing items and call out anything that might not be perfect about your listed item. Package well and ship quickly. This is the way you get good feedback. Give your buyer good feedback right away so they will want to leave feedback for you. Leaving feedback is not required so do not email and badger anyone into leaving feedback. I do not leave nasty feedback, even though I had good reason with a few buyers. You do not want bad feedback left for you. Be honest, but do watch what you post. A few times, I have just left no feedback. My 12-year experience has been very positive and profitable.

When you are comfortable using eBay and PayPal, choose the merchandise you want to sell.   Find something that you can easily acquire at low or wholesale prices. Before buying your merchandise, research eBay sales very carefully. Enter the keywords to find your product or products that are similar. When you are signed into your account (you cannot see this if you are not a member) search on the item you are interested in selling. Scroll down looking at the left side panel until you see "completed listings." Select "completed listings" to see what has sold recently and the price. Unsold items are listed in red and sold items are listed in green. Thoroughly research anything you want to sell so you can get a good idea of the selling price. If only one item sold and 50 others did not, do not choose to sell that item. You will have to compete with the other sellers listed.   You may find your idea for merchandise is not something you can make money selling or that absolutely no one is buying that item. In that case, move on to your next merchandise idea. You will save a lot of time and money by researching your merchandise first.

Income

There is no real average for people selling on eBay. Some of the published figures for yearly income range from $40,000 to $59,000 for a full-time eBay seller. Some make a very good living and others make extra money. Start out slow until you see how eBay works. Do a lot of research before you buy inventory. EBay has become a bargain hunters shopping site so do not expect retail prices but do expect windfalls on unusual items.

Etsy

Etsy.com is an online marketplace where people can buy and sell handmade, vintage items, and supplies. Sellers sign up to have a shop on Etsy where they can sell their goods. Most items are handmade with the exception of supplies to make and create projects. Sellers can also advertise to make custom orders for their customers.

If you are creative, this is the place for you to sell without the expense of having your own website. Etsy supplies your shop, customization of the look of your shop just as if you had your own website and submits your listings to search engines, which allows a lot more people to find your goods than what you might find at a local show. Etsy supplies all of the software to make your store for a very small listing fee. At this time, the listing fee is only 20 cents per item, no matter how expensive, for 4 months. There is no fee to register and join. You are charged a 3.5% fee if your item sells. This is not an auction site like eBay but similar to your own website store.

The craft market is now a $30 billion dollar per year market according to the Craft and Hobby Association. The association estimates that by 2015, the market will reach $40 billion dollars. This is inspiring a new breed of entrepreneurs.

Skills

While you must have a skill at handcrafting your items, market research is important. Create something unique and test the waters. Don't try to sell something that there are hundreds of and the price has dropped to nothing. Making a quality product is important in this market. Good quality photographs are imperative and sometimes will sell one person's item over another. Descriptive writing helps your sales in many ways. People want to hear a story, not just the dimensions and color of your item. They want to become connected with the artist.

Like all other sectors, the arts and crafts sector has been adversely affected by the downturn in the economy. While consumer spending has declined on certain types of arts and crafts, certain other items such as sewing goods, cake decorating and jewelry making supplies increased. People have tried to save money by making products themselves. As a result, the Do-It-Yourself market has gained significantly during this time. The trick here is to do your research and find a profitable niche that also fits what you enjoy. You might want to not only sell the goods to create items but to make kits as well. Etsy allows you to look at someone's store and see what has sold. Click on the "sold" button in the left sidebar. All of the items that have been sold will appear with a picture and the date. The only thing missing in "sold" listings is the price and you can be sure that if something is selling, there will be more available in the store portion of their site so you can easily find the price. That is a great way to do research and find out what is selling. Do not copy anyone's work but look for categories that are selling that are close to what you make.

Many of the crafters on Etsy have found a niche and make their living selling online through their Etsy store. Etsy has close to 500,000 members registered on the site and sellers from 80 different countries operate virtual stores. Crafters can communicate with each other. Many start slowly with little capitol and eventually make their living selling online. Etsy is also a great way to make money part time. The time investment is very small since Etsy furnishes your site, which frees crafters to use most of their time designing and making new items.

The main categories available in Etsy are handmade, vintage and supplies.   If you do not make any handmade goods or have antiques, you can sell supplies to others who make crafts or handmade goods.

Equipment

You will need the equipment to make your product and several other items for marketing.

- Equipment specific to your craft
- Computer
- Printer
- Internet connection
- Camera
- Shipping supplies for your products
- PayPal account

Income

Etsy member's income ranges from $300 to $180,000 a year. Use Etsy to research competitor's past income to estimate the income that can be made from items in different categories. Researching pays off by learning what will sell and what flops, before investing money and time.

Setting up your account

It is simple and free to set up an account with Etsy.

- Go online to: www.etsy.com
- Register for a free account on the home page
- Confirm your registration by checking your email and follow the directions in the email
- Log into your new Etsy account using your name and password
- Upload images, descriptions, prices, and shipping price of your items
- Choose categories for your items
- Select your shipping and payment options
- Preview your listing and fix any problems
- Push publish and your item will now be listed on Etsy.com
- When your item sells, Etsy collects 3.5% of your profits
- Receive payment through PayPal
- Ship the item

Etsy is a good place to sell handmade goods. People are looking for something unusual and not mass produced. Etsy is large and your work will be competing against other hand-made items. The listing price is low at 20 cents per item for 4 months and is renewable at the same rate. Five photos per item are allowed at no extra charge. Etsy submits your store to the search engines, which leads to more traffic, resulting in more sales. Personalize your store with a banner and an "about me" page. Your store will resemble a website. Payments are received through PayPal. There is a lot of competition on Etsy. Research to learn if what you want to sell is actually selling before making 20 of your items. When listing items, be sure to use descriptions and keywords that a buyer would search for to find your item.

Flea Markets

Many people make their living at flea markets. You can sell items you purchased for resale or goods you produce yourself. Location for your spot is one of the most important aspects of selling at a flea market. Try to get a prime spot where shoppers can see you when they enter the market. Sell your goods at the larger busy flea markets.

Skills

You must be a people person to sell in a flea market. Be ready to sell as soon as the doors open. The first hour and the last hour before the flea market closes are when vendors should expect to make the bulk of their earnings. Keep your tables full and well organized. Replenish the products as they sell. An empty table will turn buyers away since it looks like the table has been picked over. There should be space for customers to walk around your tables and not feel crowded. Keep your items clean and your display colorful. Your products should be clearly priced. Some people will prefer to haggle but they want to know the starting price. You will lose sales if your merchandise is not priced. Customers will walk by and others will guess the price is higher than it is. Use new price tags since old dirty tags will make the quality of your merchandise look less attractive.   Stay with your booth or you will miss sales. Display the higher priced items in front. Be friendly and available for questions but do not hover over your customers.

Equipment

You may need a truck and trailer to haul your goods to the flea market. You will need tables and racks to show off your merchandise. If you have large tables and racks to haul, you will need enough room in your truck or trailer to hold everything.

- Truck, Van, or SUV
- Trailer
- Tables
- Racks
- Bags
- Price Tags

Make sure you have an adequate supply of money for change. You should have a few hundred in twenties, tens, fives, and ones, plus at least twenty dollars in change. You can sell new items or used items. Some people sell goods they have made like picture frames, leather goods, or art. Be sure to have plastic bags since your customers may buy several items. Save grocery bags and use these, or hopefully you will sell enough merchandise to make it necessary to purchase more bags than you have saved. It is very inconvenient to walk around the market balancing goods with your hands full making it difficult to look at anything else. Having no bags may actually be a factor in someone deciding not to buy your goods. Most sell for cash, but if you are selling expensive products, you may want a portable merchant card machine.

Income

Your income will depend on the area where you live and the activity of the flea market where you are selling. The location of your booth also has a direct affect on your income. Do your research well before starting this business. What is selling, new or used items? Some people buy at auctions or buy the contents of storage units where the rent has not been paid and resell the goods. You can make $1,000 or more a weekend if you are selling merchandise that is in demand. If you are selling high dollar items, you may make $2,000 or more.

NOTE: Please refer to my websites for business resources, books, courses, software, equipment and supplies for the businesses in this book.   From time to time additional business opportunities will be posted on my website. I hope this information makes the research for your new business easier. Clicking on the links in the websites will take you to resources for each item.

http://www.pdsloss.com/
http://www.RealisticHomeBusinesses.com/

Chapter 15

How To Structure Your Business

This chapter explains the different ways you can structure your new business. You should check with your tax consultant, accountant or possibly get legal advice. Your taxes are determined by the IRS rules for each business entity. This section is an overview and not meant to be legal advice.

Business Structures

When beginning a business, you must decide what form of business entity to establish. The most common forms of business are the sole proprietorship, partnership, corporation, and S corporation. A Limited Liability Company (LLC) is a relatively new business structure allowed by state statute. Legal and tax considerations enter into selecting a business structure. You must decide which type of business structure works best with your tax situation. You should make an informed decision by consulting with a Certified Public Accountant, Accountant, or Tax Attorney.

Sole Proprietorship

A sole proprietorship is owned by one individual and is unincorporated. It is the simplest form of business organization. There is no separate existence from the owner and all of the liabilities of the business are the owner's personal liabilities. If the owner experiences a financial crisis, the business assets are also at risk. The income and expenses of the business are included on the owner's individual tax return. It is a good idea to have business insurance or errors and omissions insurance depending on the type of business you select. Schedule C of the federal income tax return allows all expenses of the business to be deducted before the remainder is passed along as income on the individual's return.

Partnership

A partnership is the relationship existing between two or more persons who join to carry on a trade or business. Each person contributes money, property, labor or skill, and expects to share in the profits and losses of the business. A partnership must file an annual return to report the income, deductions, gains, losses, etc., from its operations, but it does not pay income tax. Instead, it "passes through" any profits or losses to its partners. Each partner includes their share of the partnership's income or loss on their tax return. Partners are not employees and should not be issued a Form W-2. The partnership must furnish copies of Schedule K-1 to the partners.

Corporation

In forming a corporation, prospective shareholders exchange money, property, or both, for the corporation's capital stock. A corporation generally takes the same deductions as a sole proprietorship to figure its taxable income. A corporation can also take special deductions. For federal income tax purposes, a C corporation is recognized as a separate taxpaying entity. A corporation conducts business, realizes net income or loss, pays taxes and distributes profits to shareholders.

The profit of a corporation is taxed to the corporation when earned, and then is taxed to the shareholders when distributed as dividends. This creates a double tax. The corporation does not get a tax deduction when it distributes dividends to shareholders. Shareholders cannot deduct any loss of the corporation.

C Corporation

A C corporation is a standard business corporation. It is unlikely that you would start a small business as a C corporation. A C corporation is taxed under subsection C of the IRS code. There may be an unlimited number of shareholders in a C corporation. The shareholders of a C corporation may include other corporations, LLCs, individuals, trusts or partnerships. A shareholder of a C corporation need not be a citizen of the U.S. or a resident for that matter. Many states allow a single person to form and operate a C corporation.

A major benefit provided by a C corporation is limited liability. The shareholders of a C corporation have limited liability against debts and obligation incurred by the corporation. The desire to protect personal assets from business liabilities often acts as the motivating force for starting a C corporation. Business creditors of a C corporation may not pursue the personal assets of its shareholders in an attempt to recover business debts.

All profits of a C corporation are subject to double taxation. Double taxation occurs when the profits of the C corporation are taxed on the business level. Shareholders of C corporations are required to pay taxes on all dividends received from the C corporation. Since the profits of the C corporation have been taxed before dividends are distributed to shareholders, the ensuing tax on shareholder dividends amounts to "double taxation" on the same corporate dollars. There are certain tax advantages gained by incorporating as a C corporation. If the C corporation keeps profits in the company, in lieu of distributing dividends, the corporate tax rate may be lower than the shareholder's individual tax rate.

S Corporation

The S corporation is designed to eliminate "double taxation" which occurs when the profits of a corporation are taxed first as income to the corporation, then again as income to the shareholders when profits are distributed as dividends.   S corporations are responsible for tax on certain built-in gains and passive income. To qualify for S corporation status, the corporation must meet the following requirements:

- Be a domestic corporation
- Have only allowable shareholders
    - including individuals, certain trust, and estates and
    - may not include partnerships, corporations or non-resident alien shareholders
- Have no more than 100 shareholders
- Have one class of stock
- Not be an ineligible corporation, i.e. certain financial institutions, insurance companies, and domestic international sales corporations.

Limited Liability Corporation (LLC)

A Limited Liability Company (LLC) is a business structure allowed by state statute. LLCs are popular because, similar to a corporation, owners have limited personal liability for the debts and actions of the LLC. Other features of LLCs are more like a partnership, providing management flexibility and the benefit of pass-through taxation. Owners of an LLC are called members.   Since most states do not restrict ownership, members may include individuals, corporations, other LLCs and foreign entities. There is no maximum number of members. Most states also permit "single member" LLCs, those having only one owner.

Some types of businesses generally cannot be LLCs, such as banks and insurance companies. Check your state's requirements and the federal tax regulations for further information. There are special rules for foreign LLCs.

Local, State and Federal Agency Information

Internal Revenue Service

Businesses other than sole proprietorships need an Employer Identification Number (EIN). An EIN is known as a federal tax identification number. I would suggest having an EIN, even for a sole proprietorship, simply to protect your social security number. That way, if you do consulting for someone who needs your social security number, the EIN can be used in its place. The income will still be tied to your social security number and you do not have to give out personal information. Here is the IRS link to get your EIN online:

http://www.irs.gov/businesses/small/article/0,,id=98350,00.html

This page will answer any questions you may have and has the following link "Apply for an EIN online". It is free, simple and you will get the number quickly.

Secretary of State

Every state has a website that handles new business start-ups. You can select your business entity from sole proprietor to one of the corporation types. You will need a trade name. There is usually a place you can search to see if a name has already been taken. It is important to file for a trade name to avoid duplication. If you shared the same name with someone who had a bad reputation, it would reflect on you. The state will not allow duplicate trade names.

Most states allow all of the paperwork to be submitted online. For example, Colorado will let you select a sole proprietor business name, pay $20.00 by credit card and immediately be able to print your new business trade name documents out on a printer. Your trade name must be renewed annually, which can be done online. The current rate for Colorado is $5.00 a year.

You can open a business bank account using your business name if you have registered with the state. Banks can verify your documents in minutes by checking your state's website. Some banks require a copy of your trade name documents. It is also important to file for a trade name to avoid having the same business name as someone else.

State Tax License

If you are selling a product or buying for resale, you will need a state tax license. Find the state revenue office in the town where you live.   In the front of your phone book, you will find listings for "city", "county", and "state".   The listing should be under state revenue. Normally, you must appear in person with your state trade name papers in hand for your new business. You may be charged a deposit and a fee for the tax license. Your deposit will be refunded after a dollar amount of tax is paid. Each state is different but the process should be the same. The state also collects taxes for the city and county where your business is located and distributes tax funds to each entity. One tax license is all you need. Check with your state and get the correct tax license since some states may operate differently.

County Clerk

Contact your County Clerk's office to see if registration in your county is required as well. You may need to register your business name or DBA (Doing Business As) name.

Names and Trademarks

New Business Name

When you search online for your business name with your Secretary of State and County Clerk, you will have to make sure no one else is already using your proposed business name. If your name is not available, it will be necessary to create a new name or variation of the name you selected.

Trademarks

If you have designed a logo to brand your business, it is desirable to trademark protect your logo. This will prevent others from using the logo that you designed for marketing your business. Make sure your logo or trademark is exclusive and is not similar to another company's design. If it is similar, make changes and modify the design before applying for a trademark. It is wise to consult a trademark lawyer to ensure your trademark logo does not infringe upon another trademarked logo before applying.

NOTE: Please refer to my websites for business resources, books, courses, software, equipment and supplies for the businesses in this book. From time to time additional business opportunities will be posted on my website. I hope this information makes the research for your new business easier. Clicking on the links in the websites will take you to resources for each item.

> http://www.pdsloss.com/
> http://www.RealisticHomeBusinesses.com/

Chapter 16

Conclusion

I hope you have benefited from the information provided in this book and have found an enjoyable and profitable home business. For business resources, classes, books, equipment, supplies, or software, please visit my website:

http://www.pdsloss.com/
http://www.RealisticHomeBusinesses.com/

Numerous resources are listed there that you may find useful. Click on the links to be taken directly to the sites. Some will have coupons for an extra percent off or free shipping when you get there from my website. I will add more as time goes on. A business blog lists business tips and new businesses that are not in this book that you might find interesting.

Getting started is the hardest part. Listed below are helpful steps to follow in finding and setting up your new business.

- Part-time or full-time decision
- Choose skills & passions
- Find your niche
- Research the business and competition
- Develop a business plan with financial forecast

- Decide if the business is feasible
- Structure and name your business
- Buy needed business resources, books, equipment, supplies, and software
- Make cards, flyers, brochures, and website if needed
- Start your new business
- Market your new business

I wish you every success in your new home business!

Index

About the Author

Pat D. Sloss is a writer and engineer with more than 30 years experience in Technical Writing, Grant/Proposal Writing, Research, Business Writing, Commercial/Aerospace Engineering, Biomedical Engineering, Teaching, Oil & Gas Management, Greenhouse Nursery, and Ranching. She has written more than 30 books and manuals for commercial, medical, and aerospace companies. Her writing skills also include successful proposals, grants, business plans, resumes, and marketing materials.

Her diverse background comes from growing up on a large mountain cattle ranch working cattle, riding horses, and being able to fix things with baling wire. She was an engineer and writer for high tech, aerospace, and medical companies.

She has either previously or currently been involved in 28 of the businesses listed. Friends and acquaintances are involved in 30 of the businesses

www.ingramcontent.com/pod-product-compliance
Lightning Source LLC
Chambersburg PA
CBHW060300100426
42742CB00011B/1819